MANDALAS HEARTS AND FLOWERS:

50 PLUS PAGES FOR STRESS RELIEVING THERAPEUTIC COLORING BOOK

Andrea Reynolds

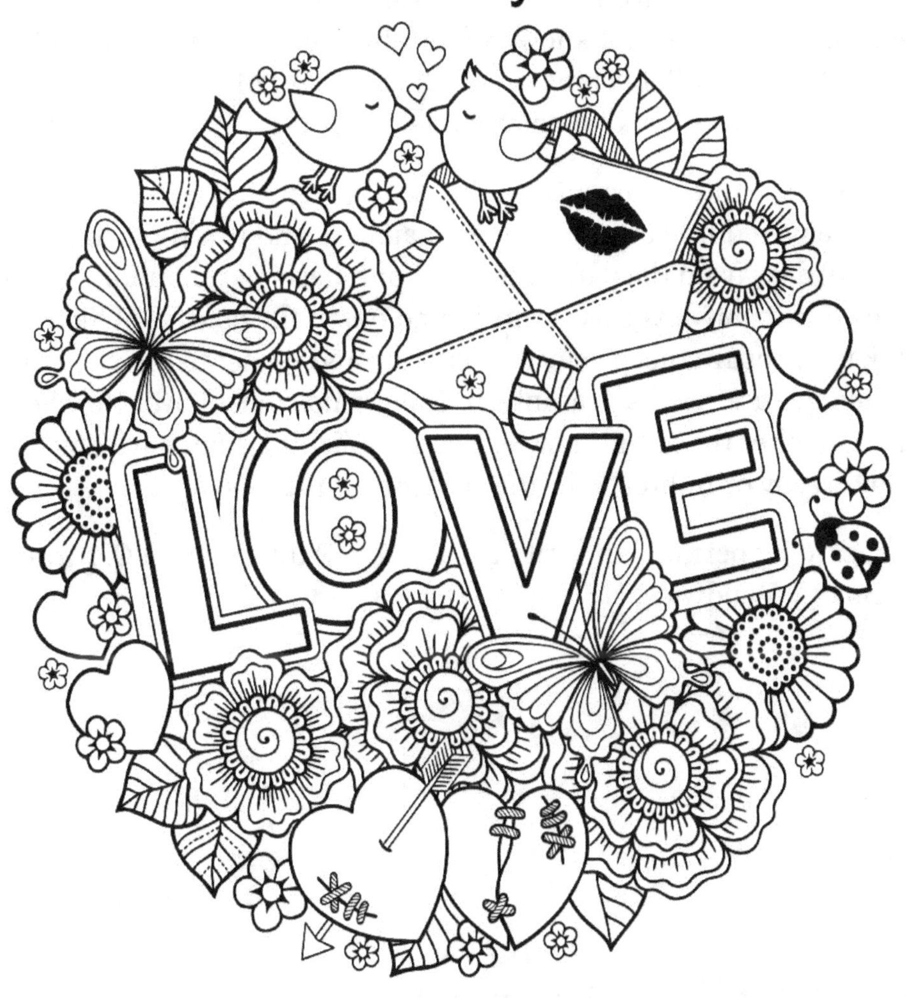

Mandalas Hearts and Flowers: 50 Plus Pages for Stress Relieving Therapeutic Coloring Book

For information regarding permission, write to: Skyshan Publishing, LLC. Att: Permissions Department, PO Box 13, Waldwick, NJ 07463

 Published by Skyshan Publishing, LLC

ISBN: 978-1-970106-44-2

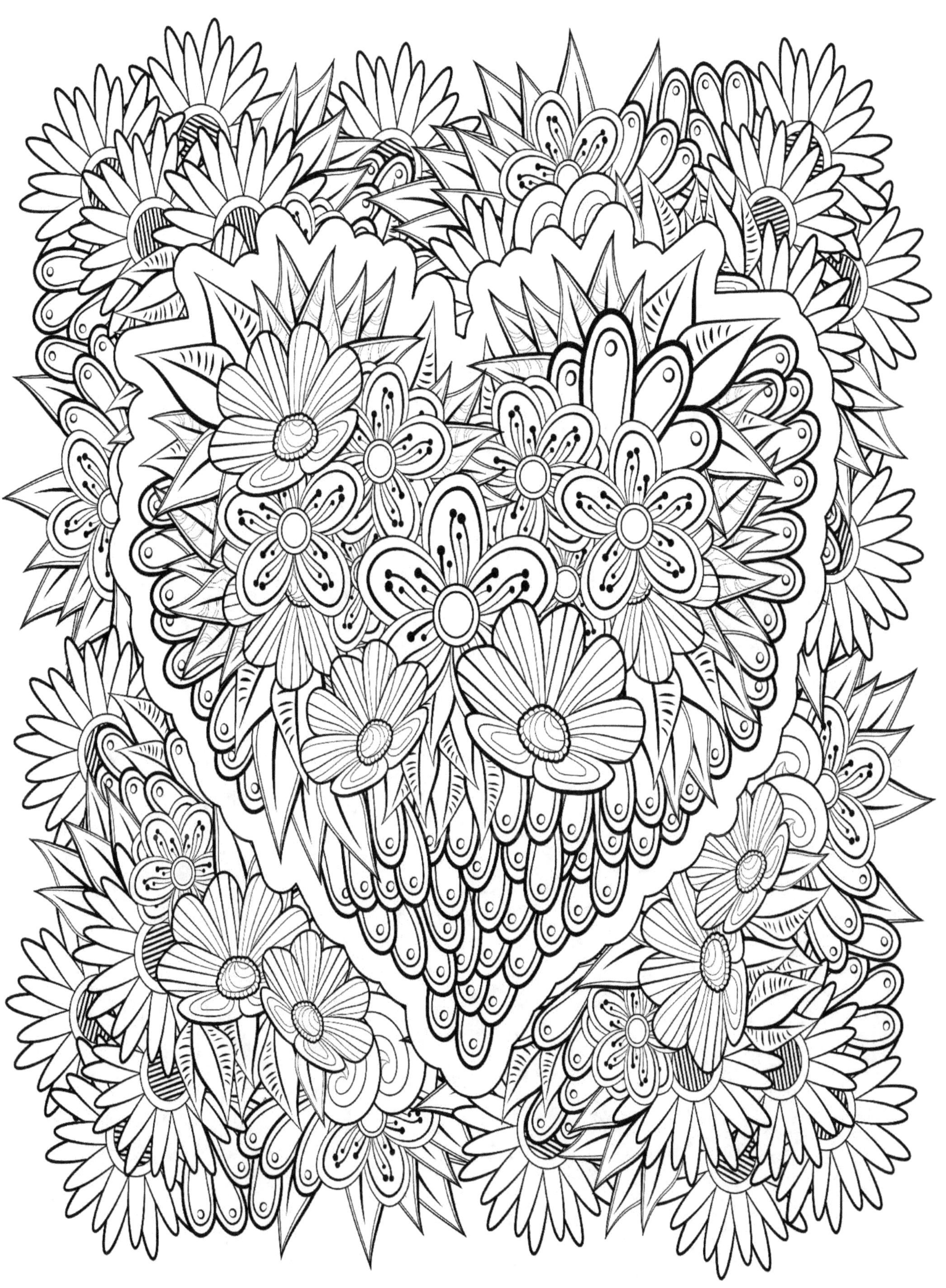

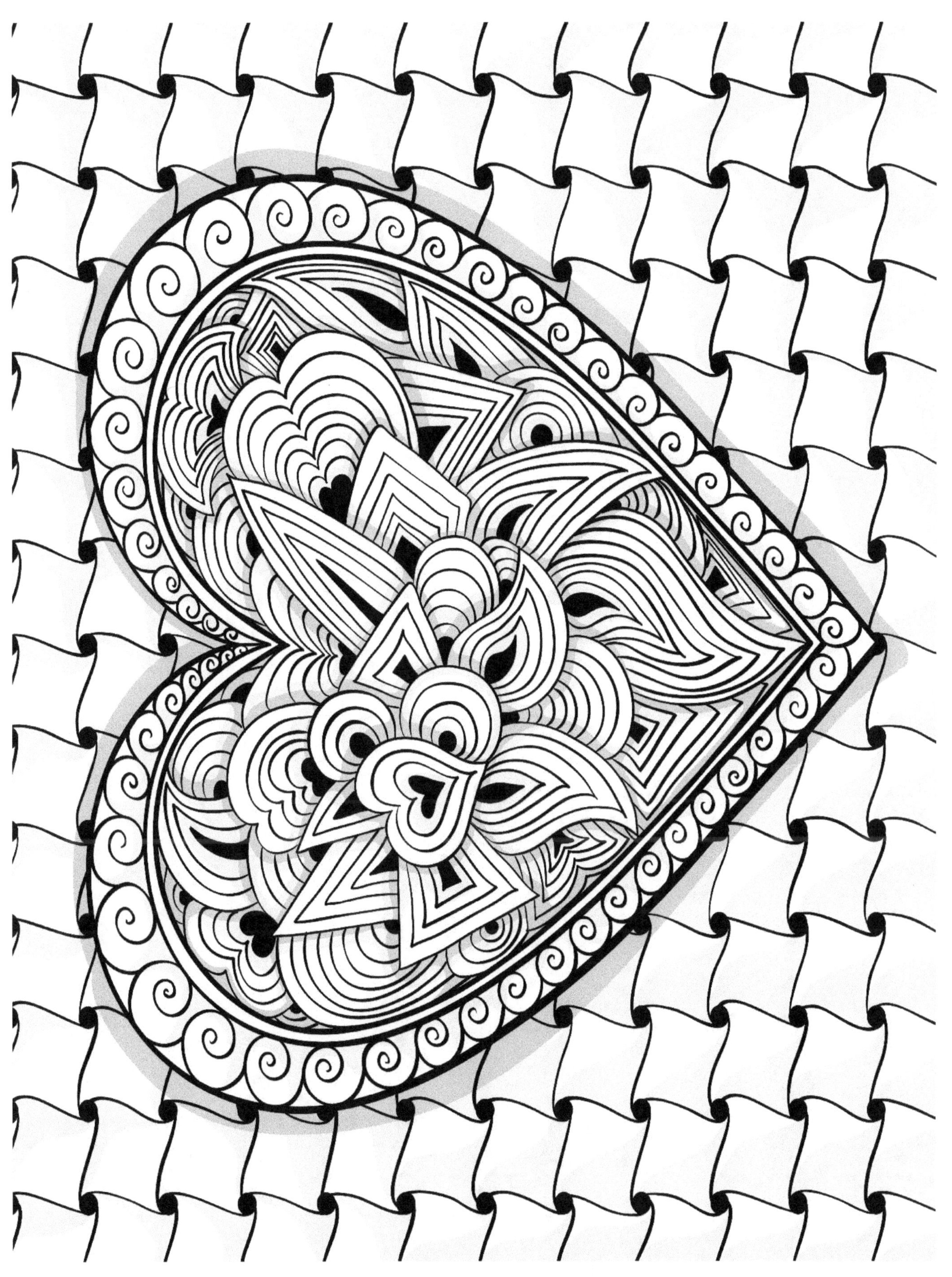

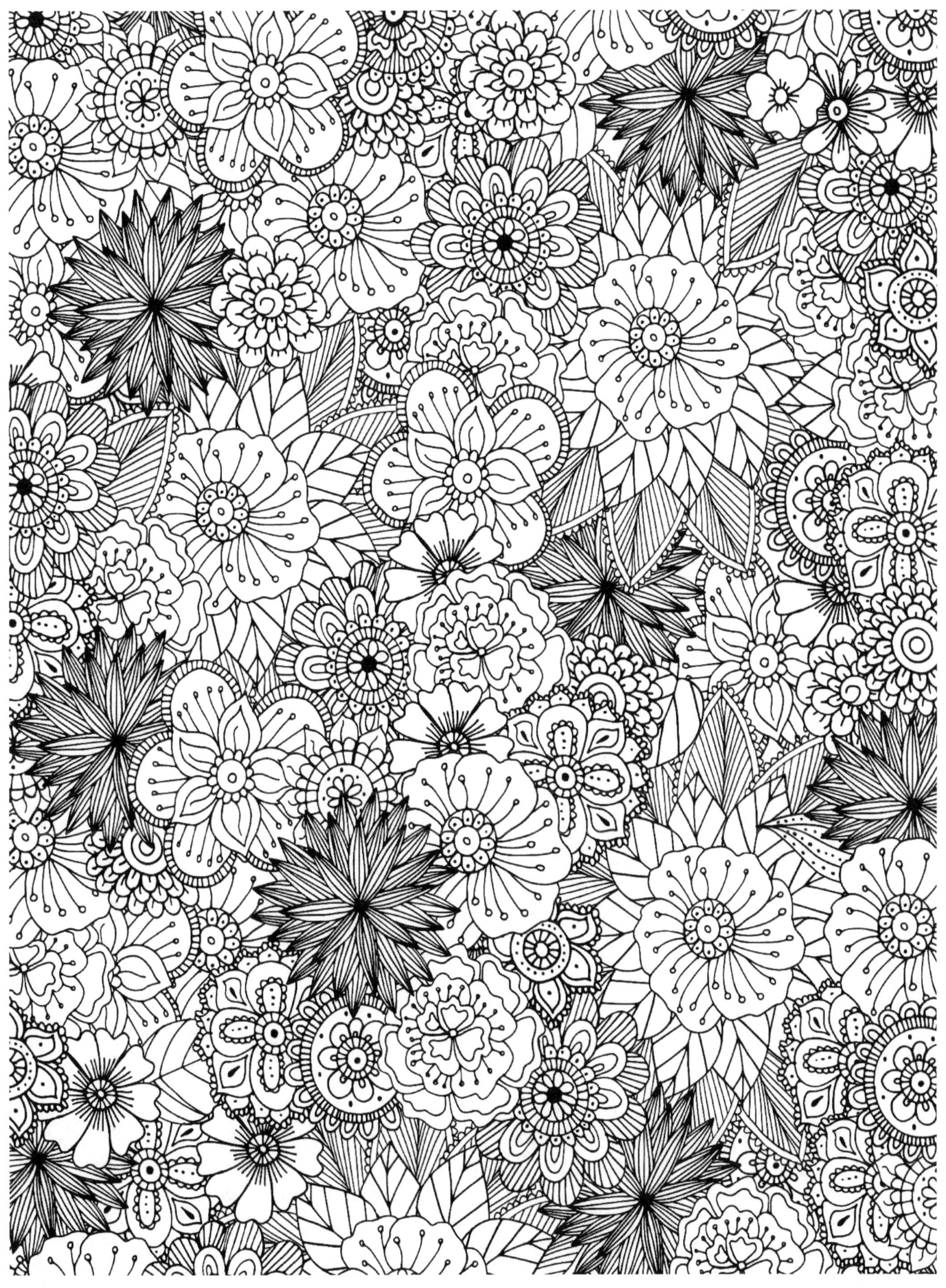

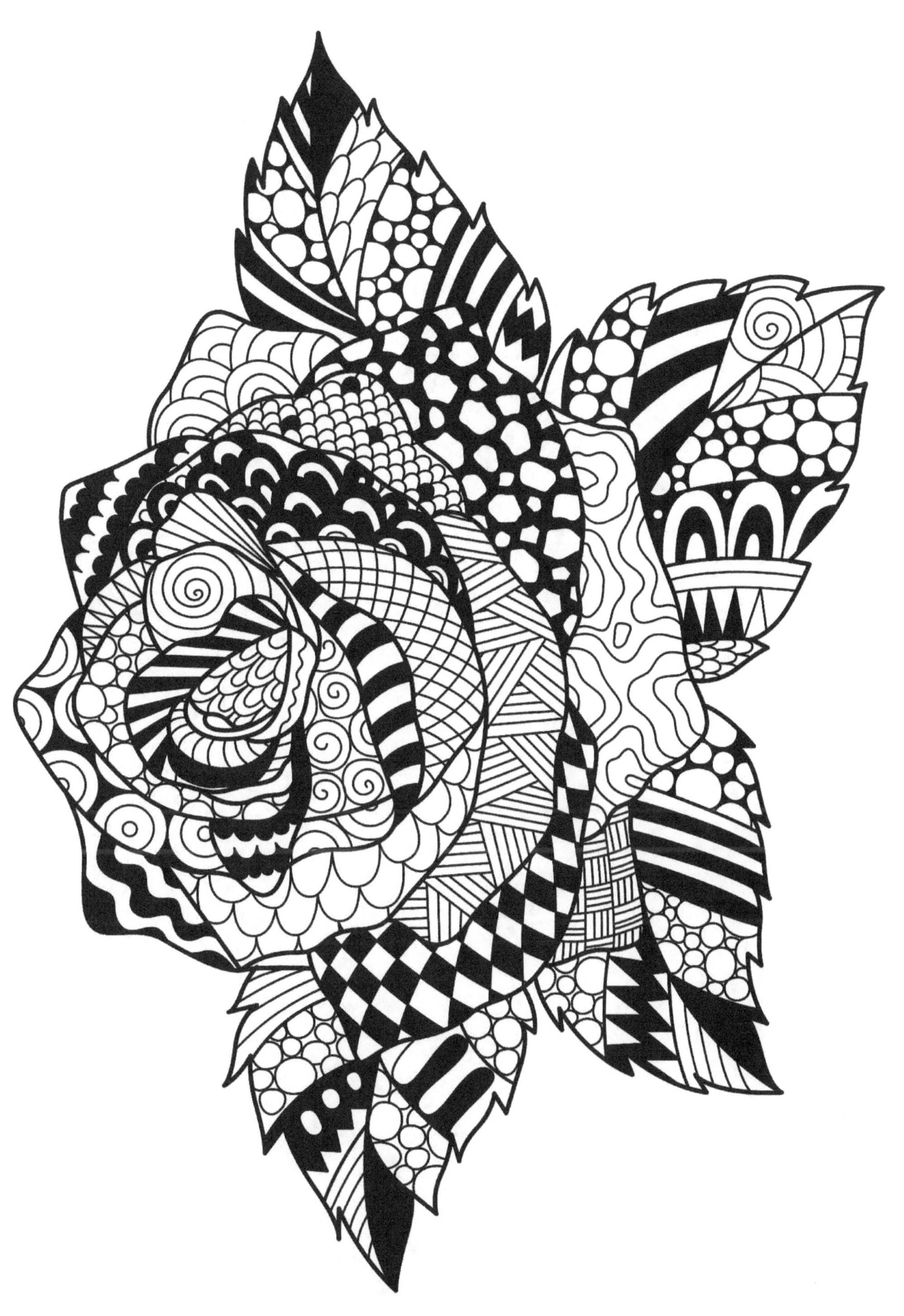

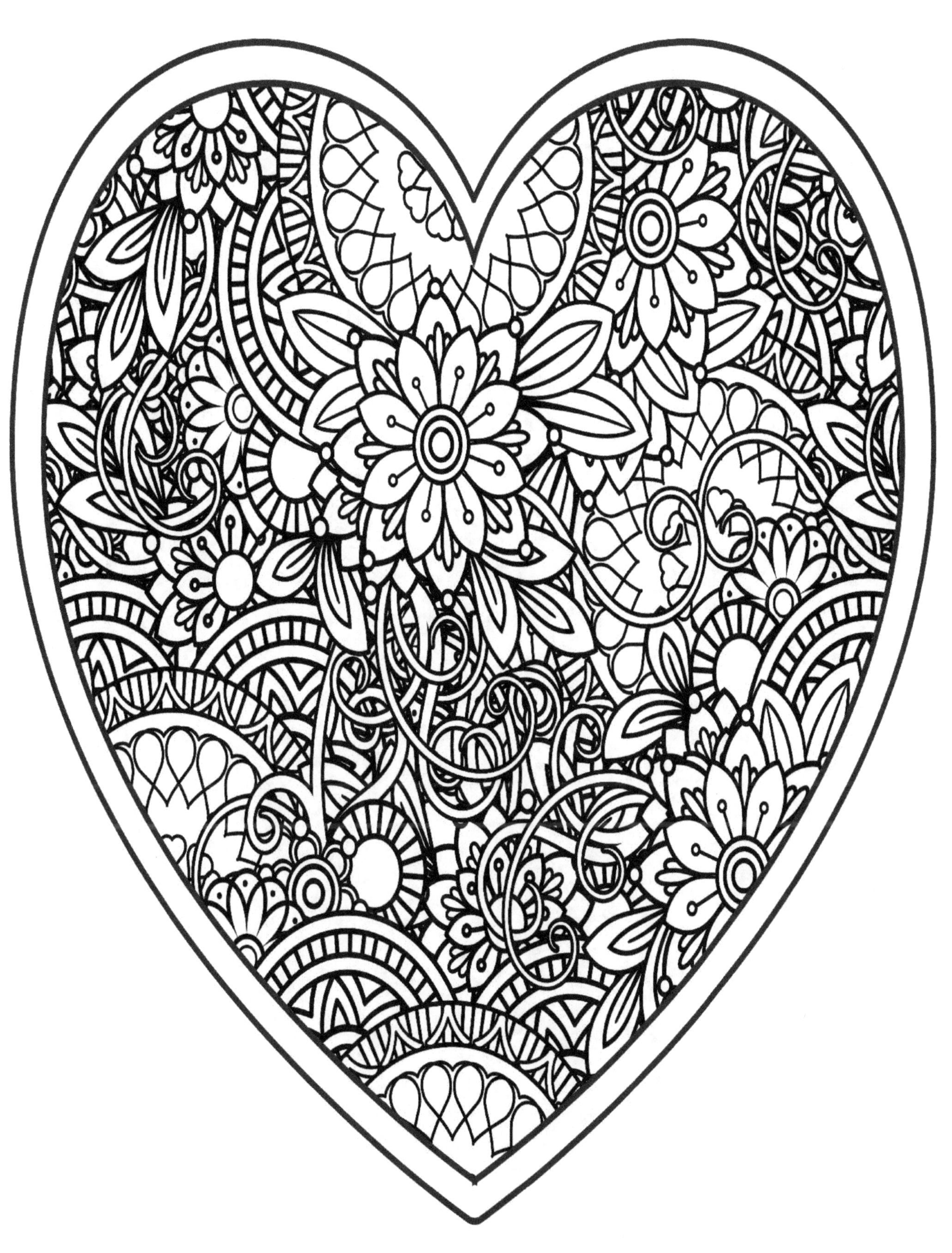

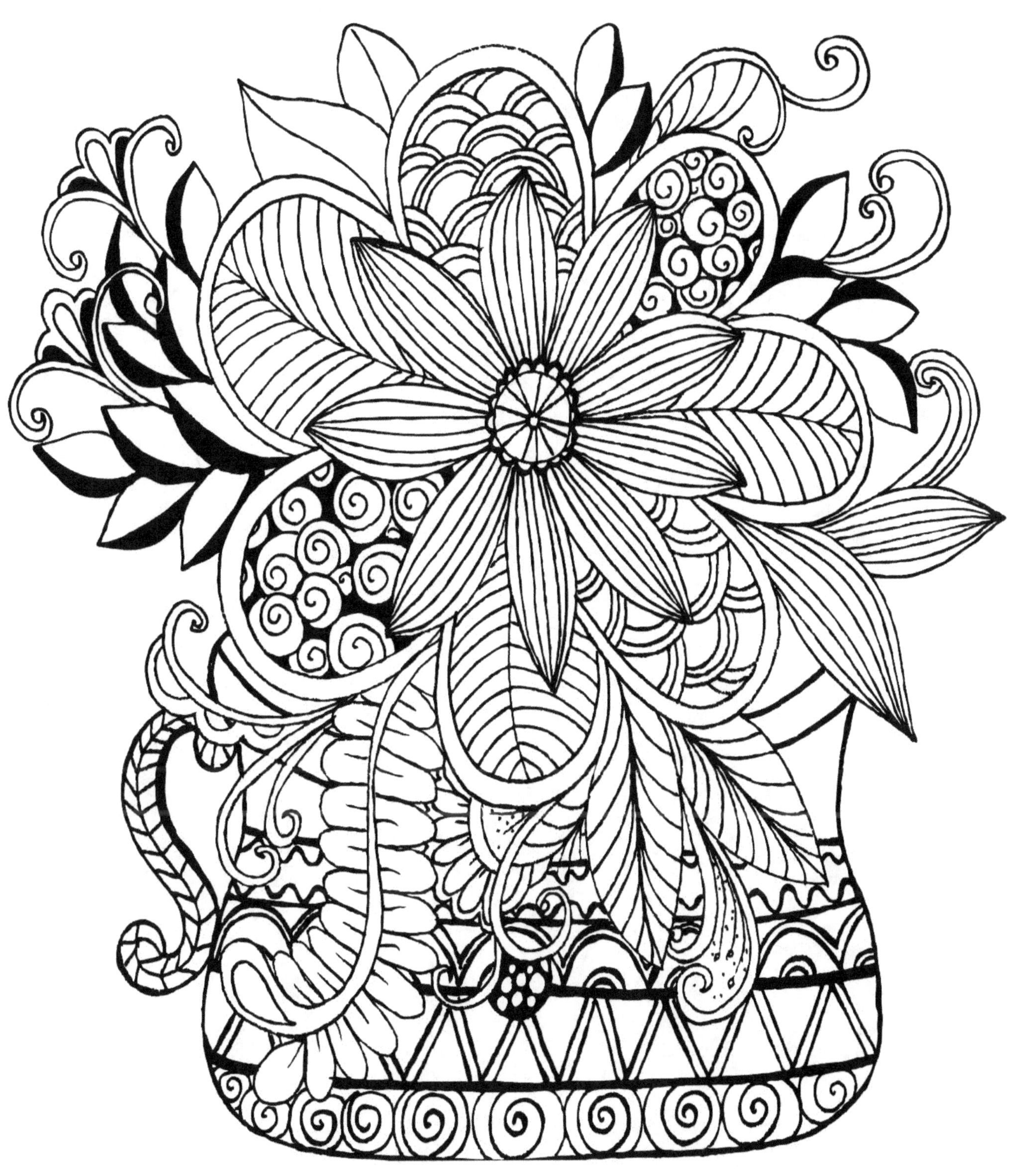

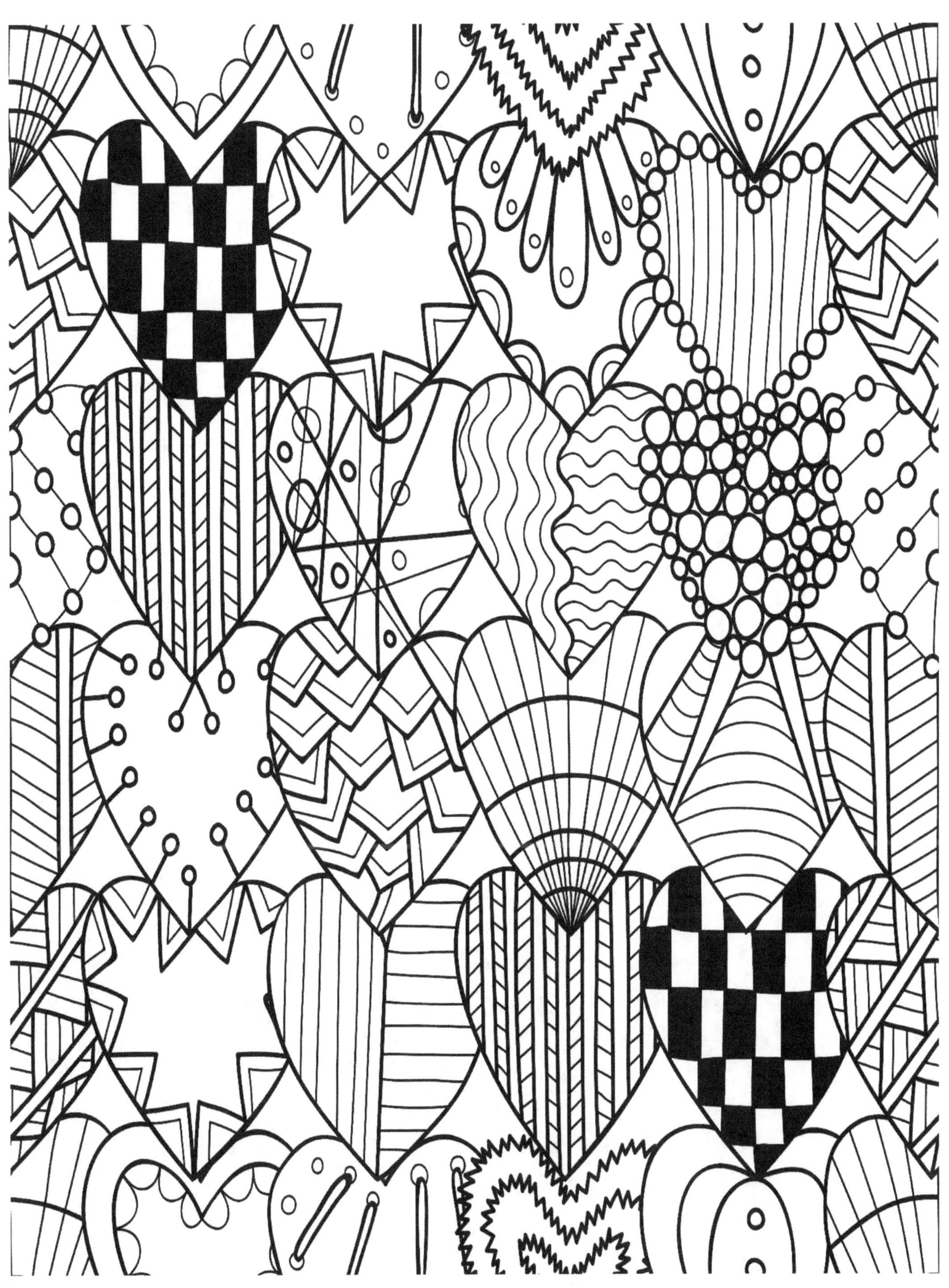

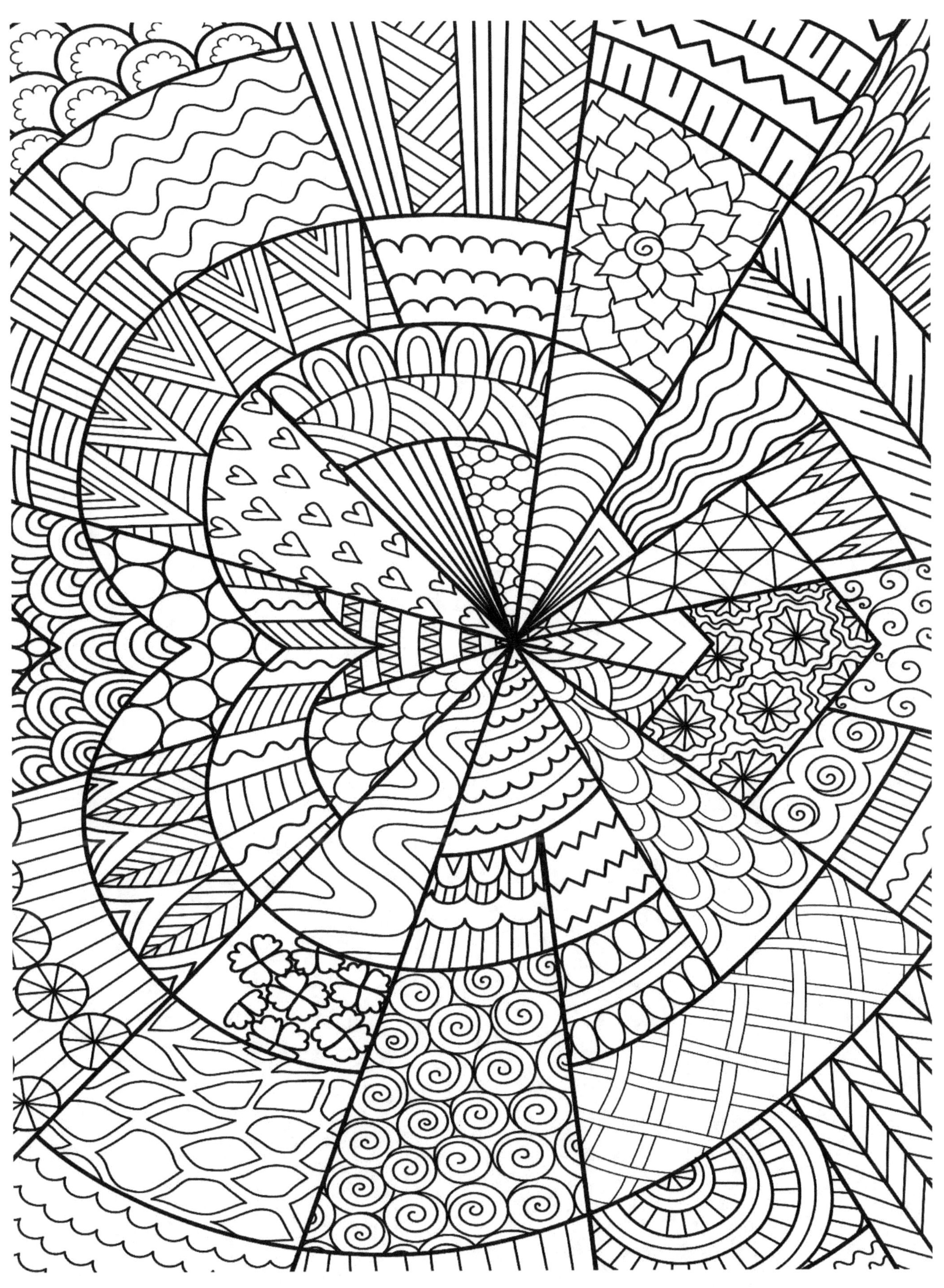

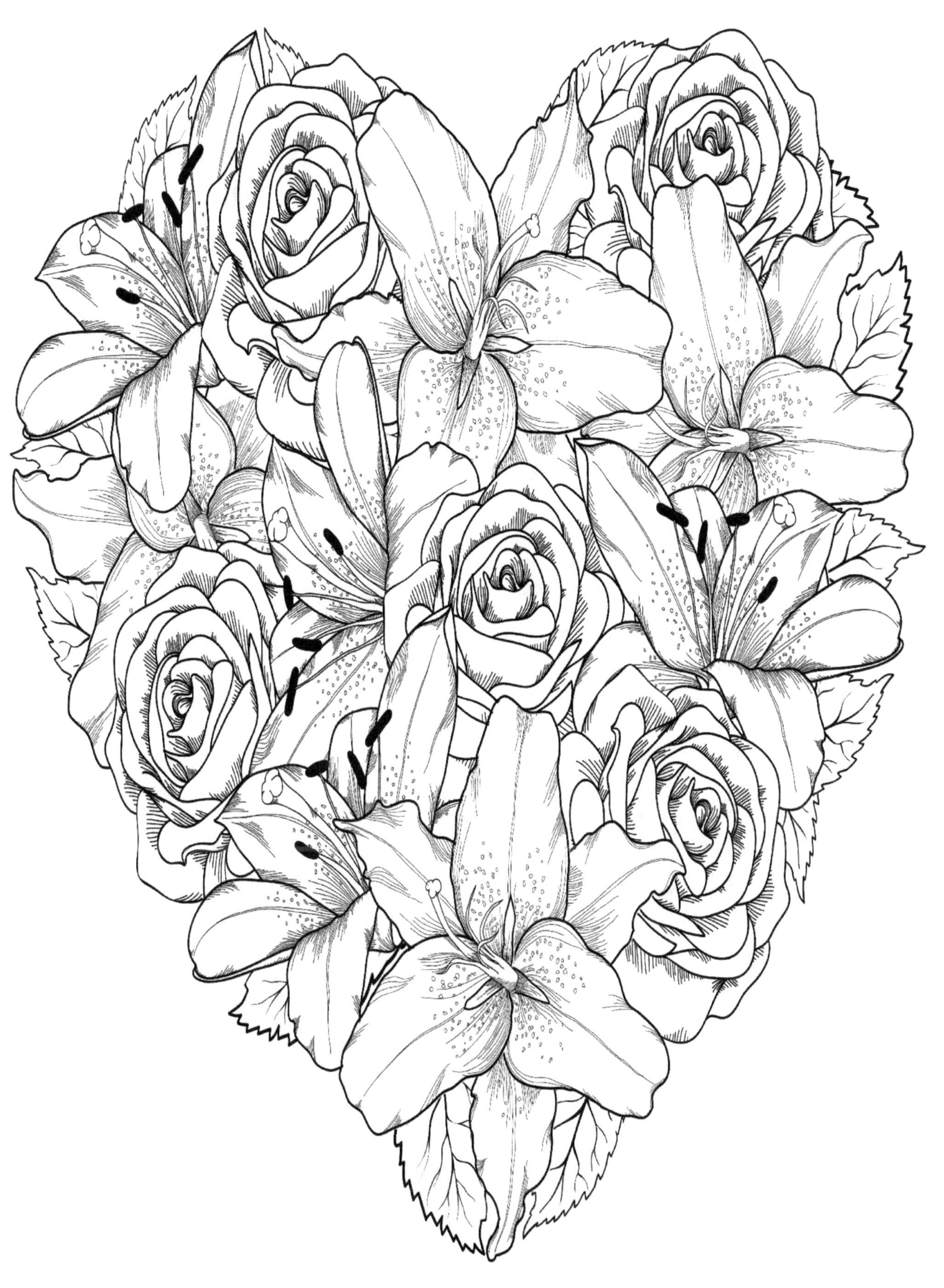

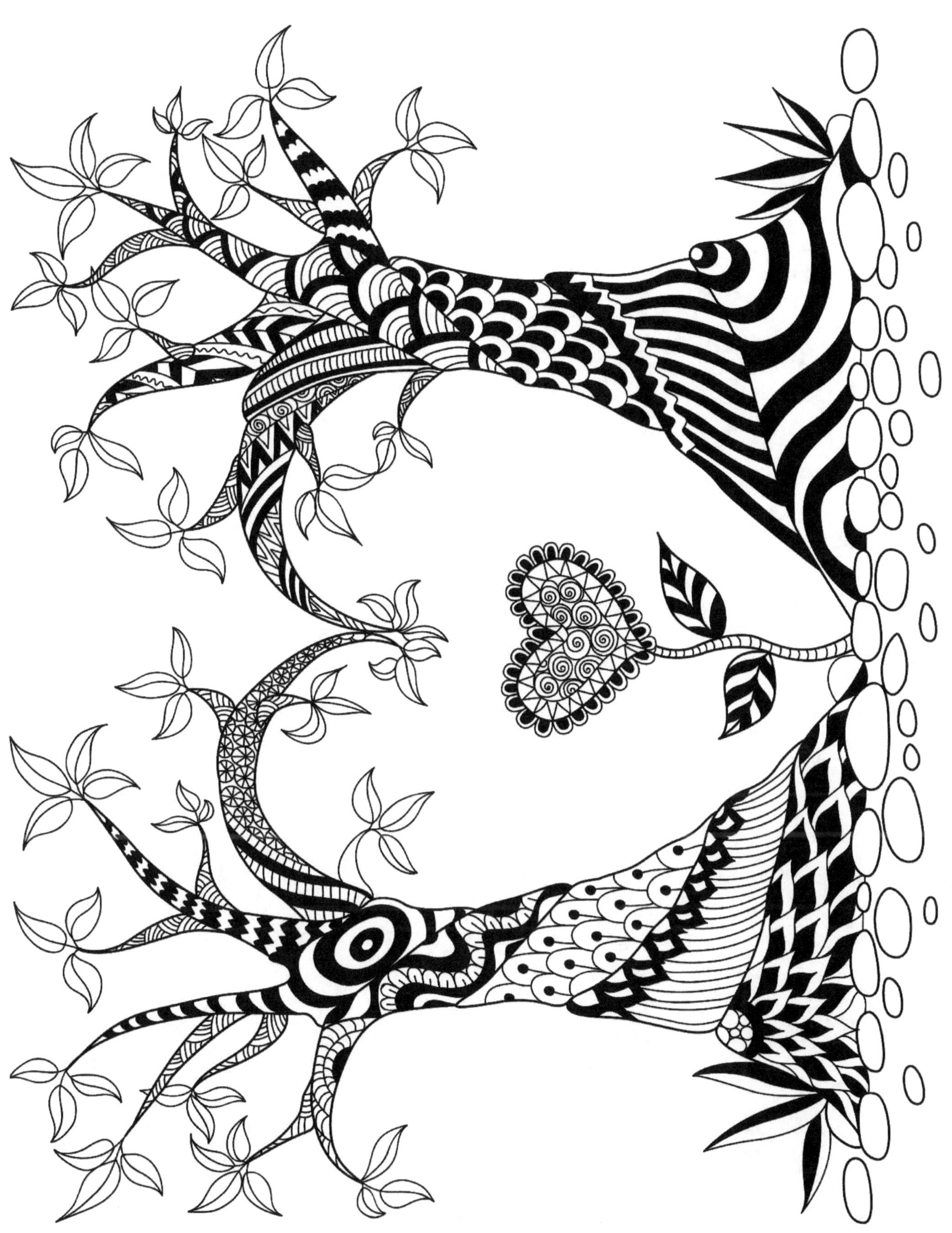

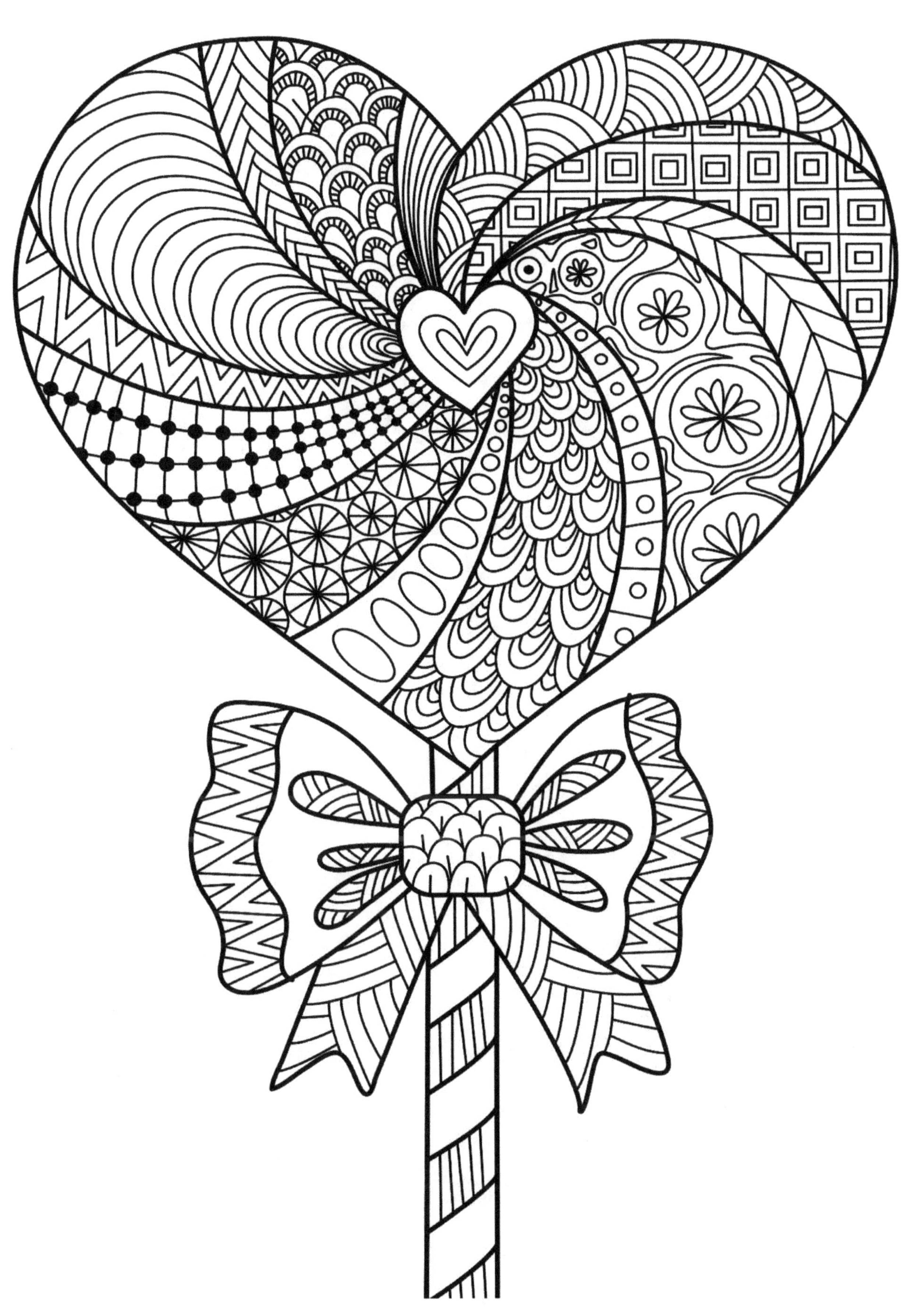

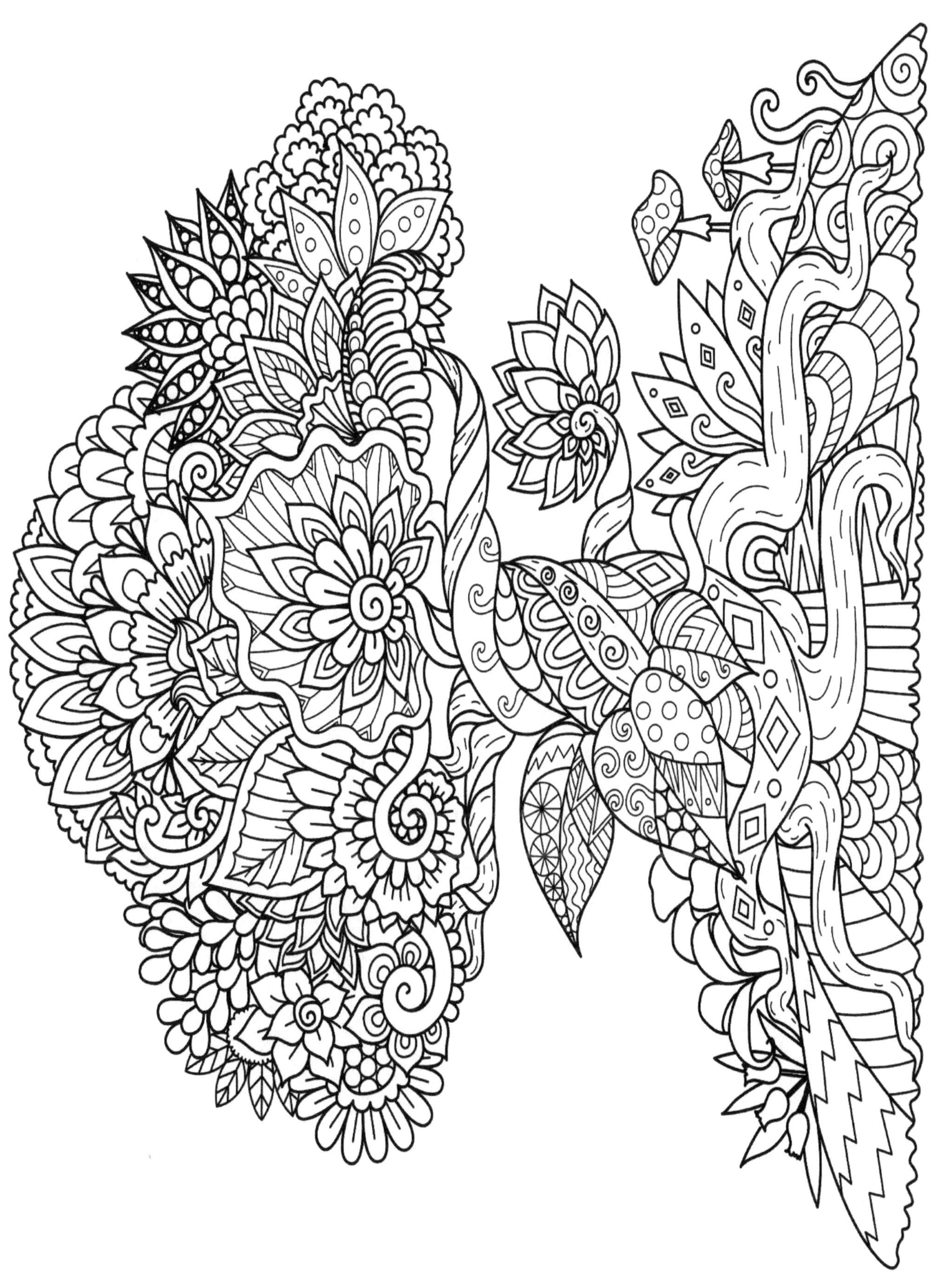

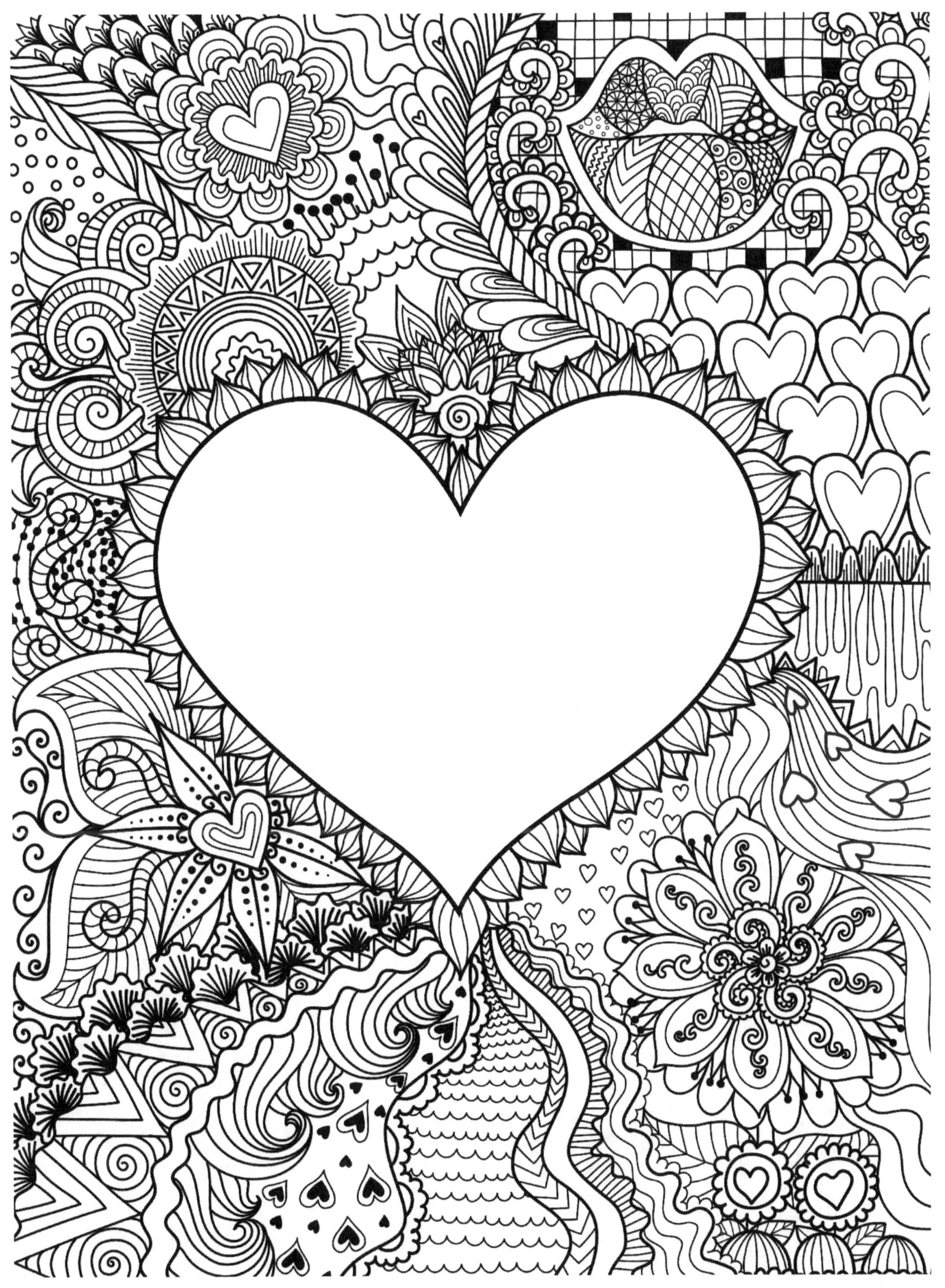

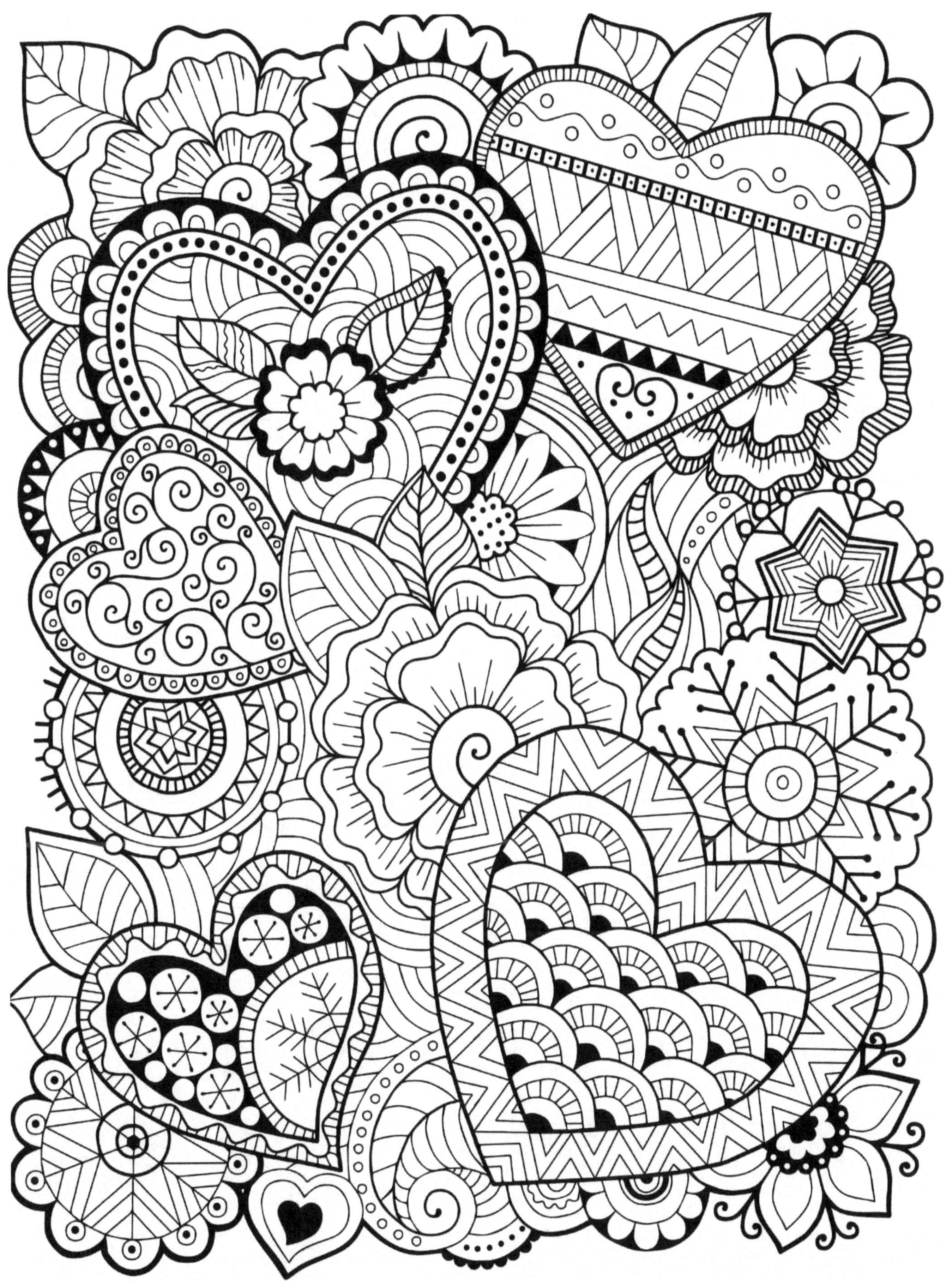

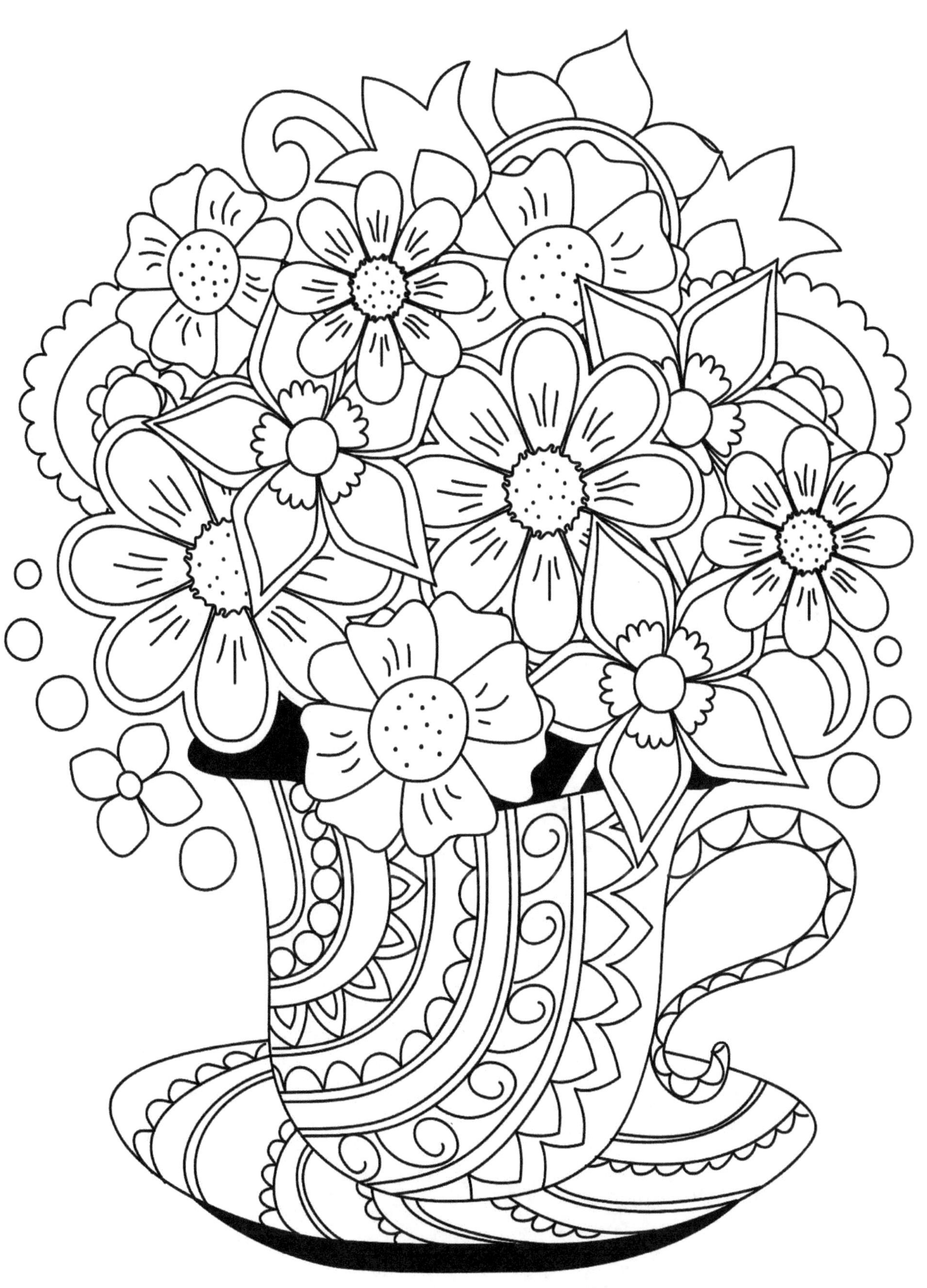

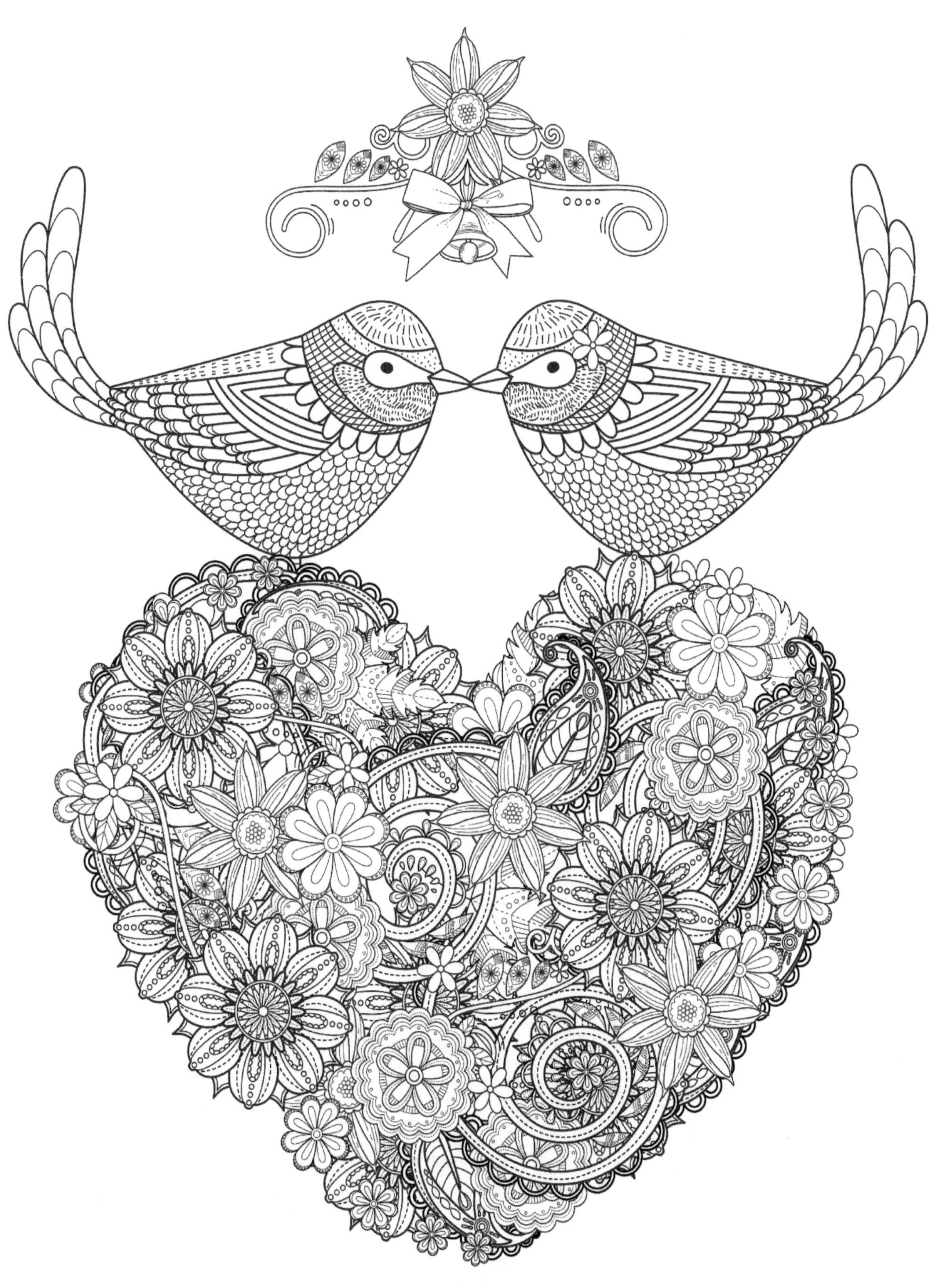

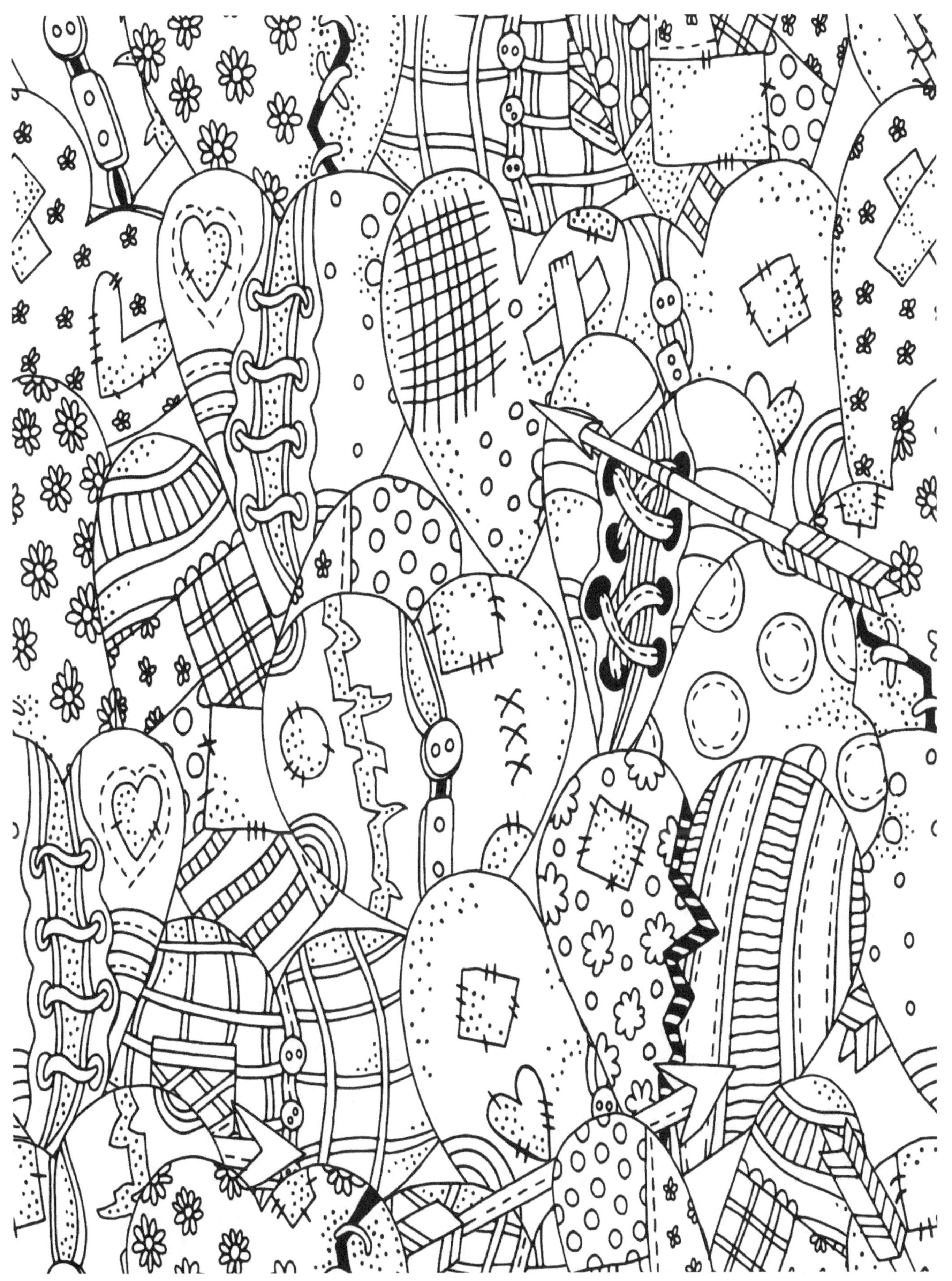

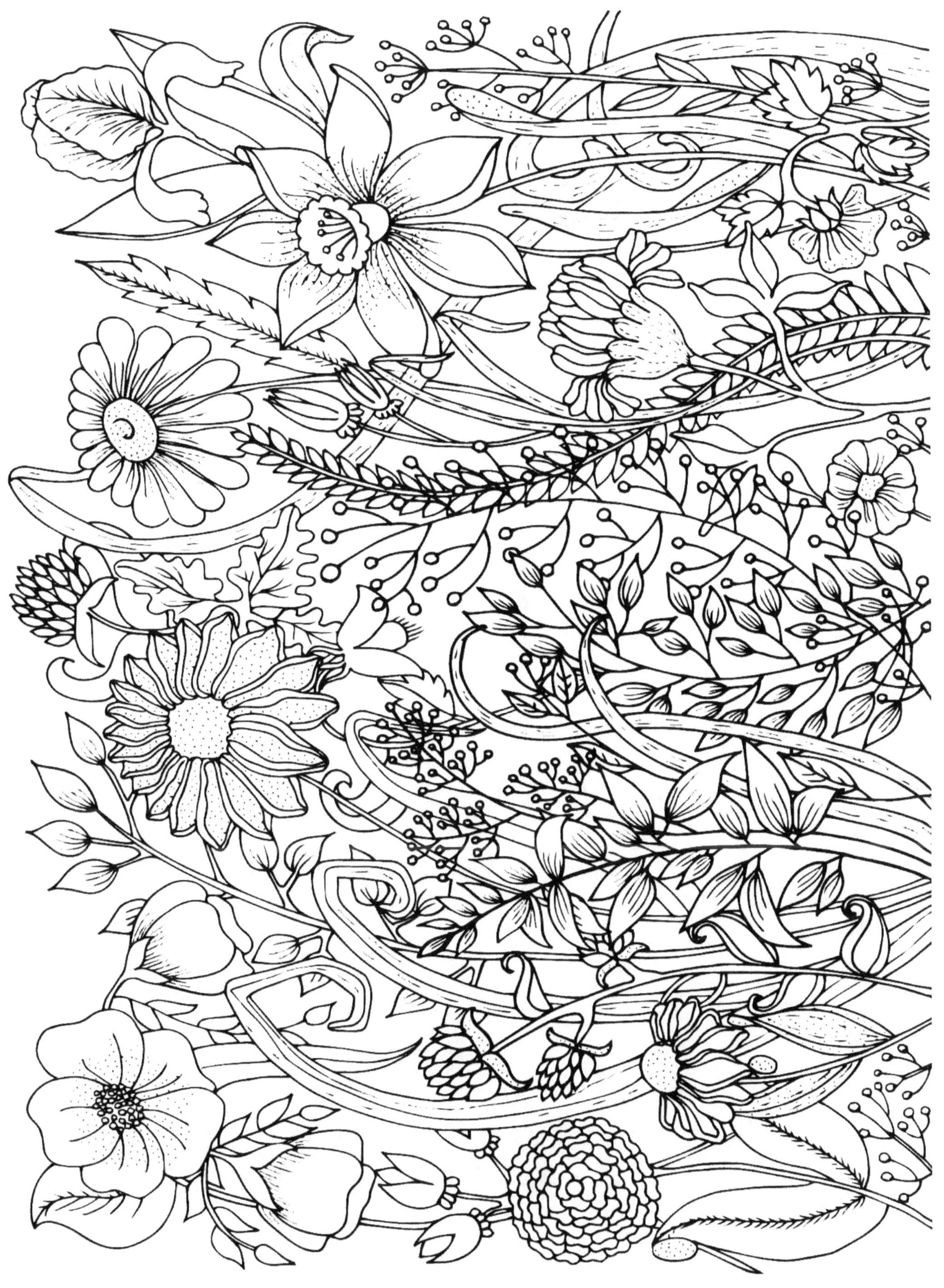

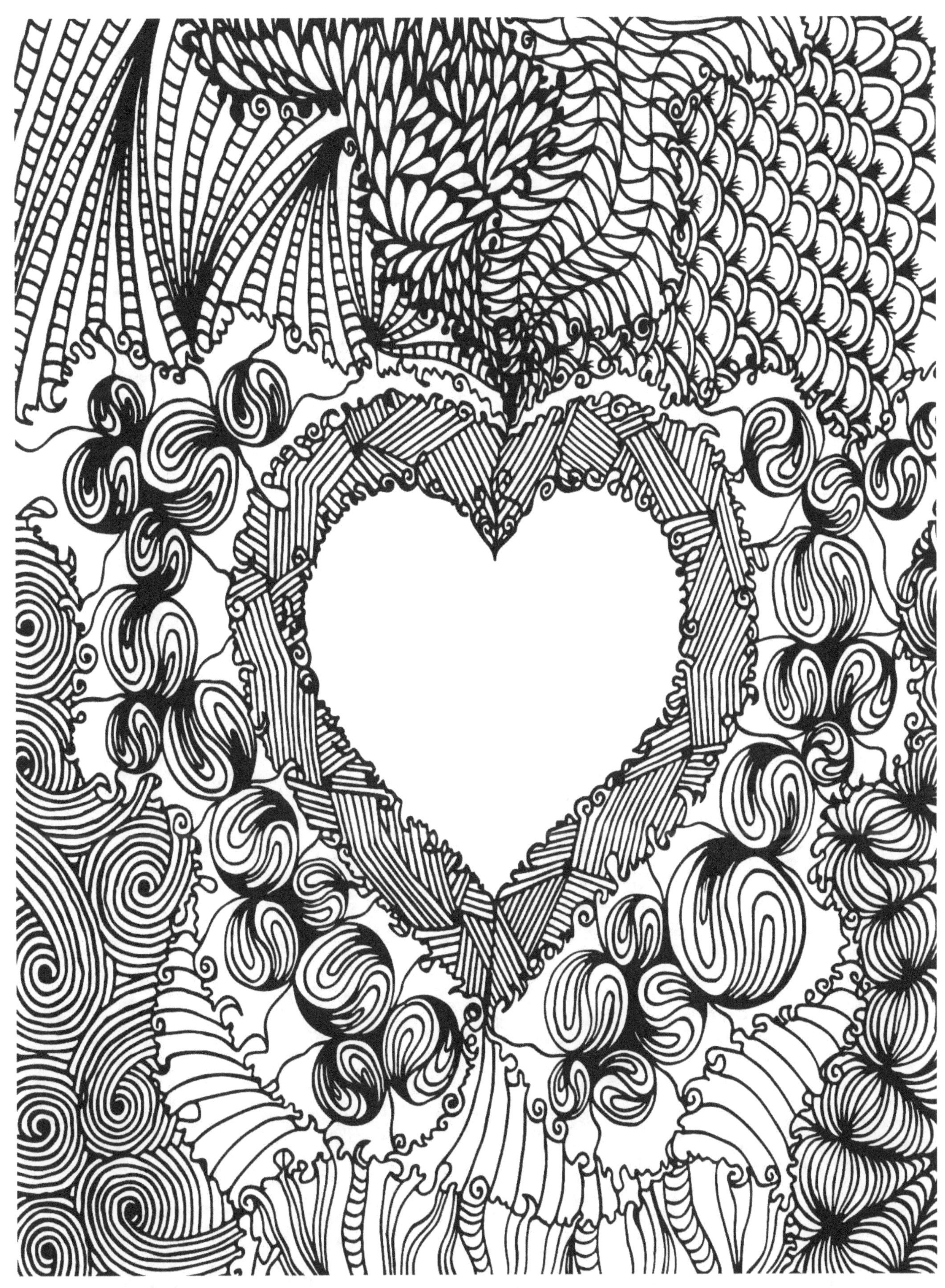

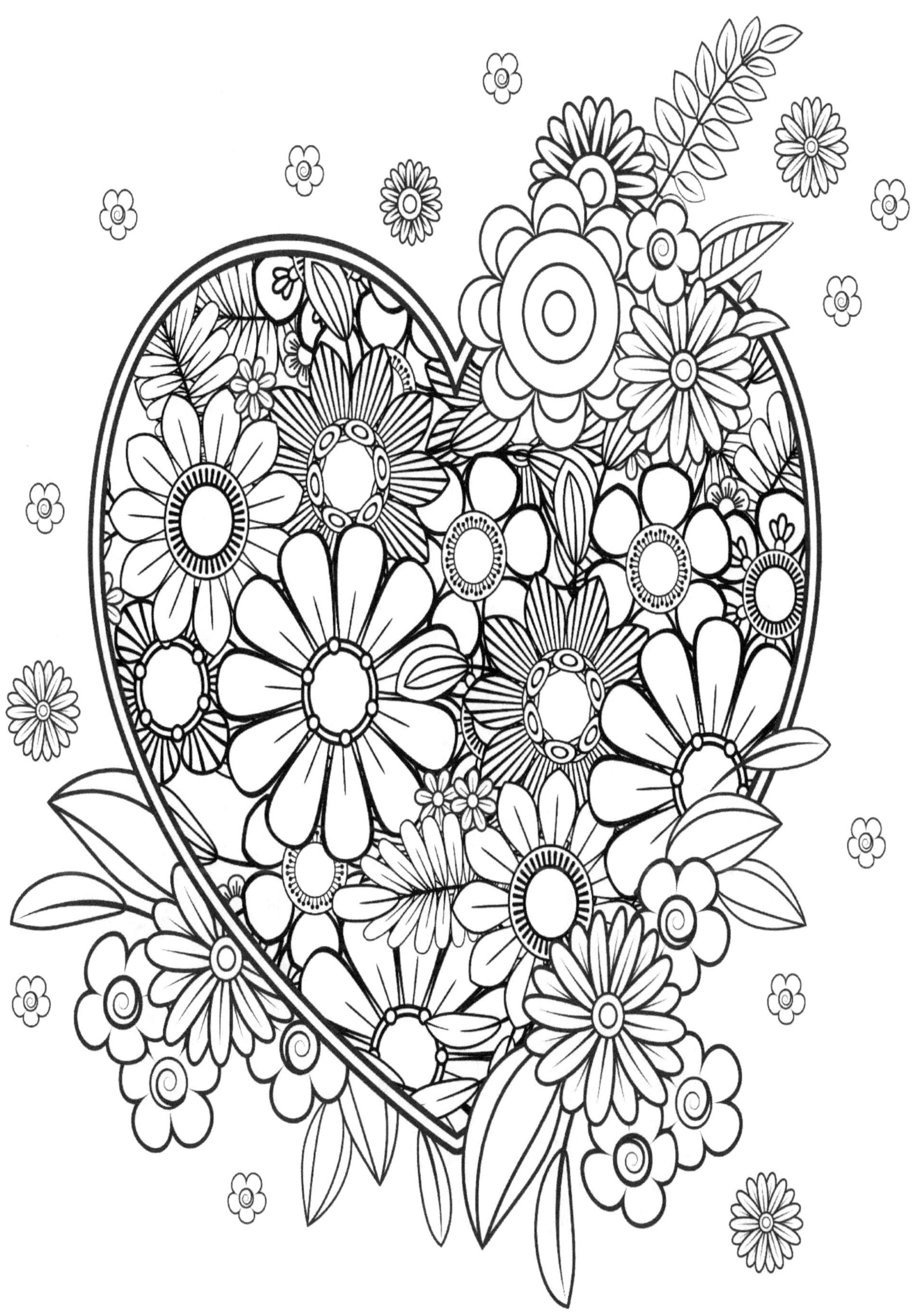

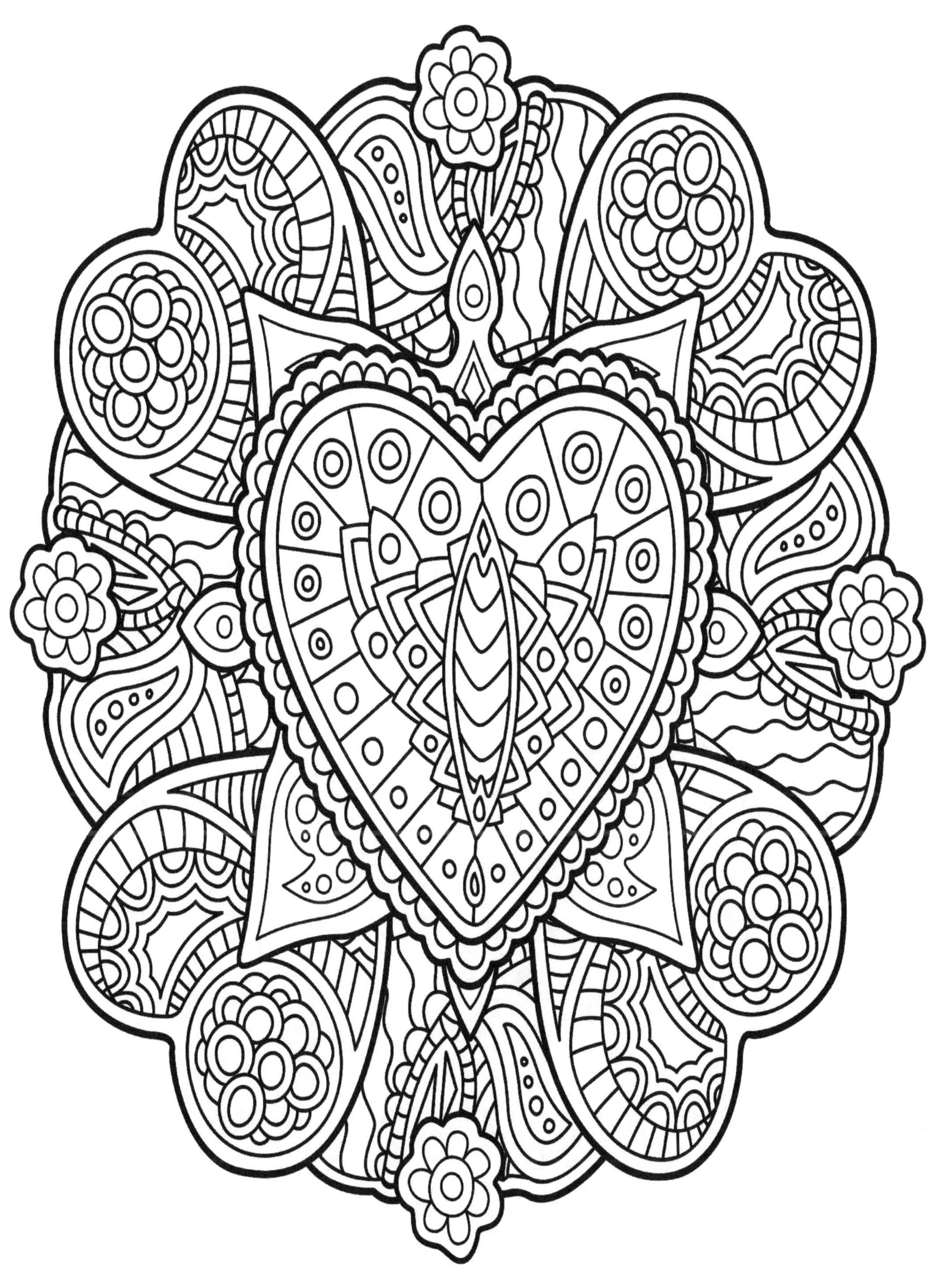

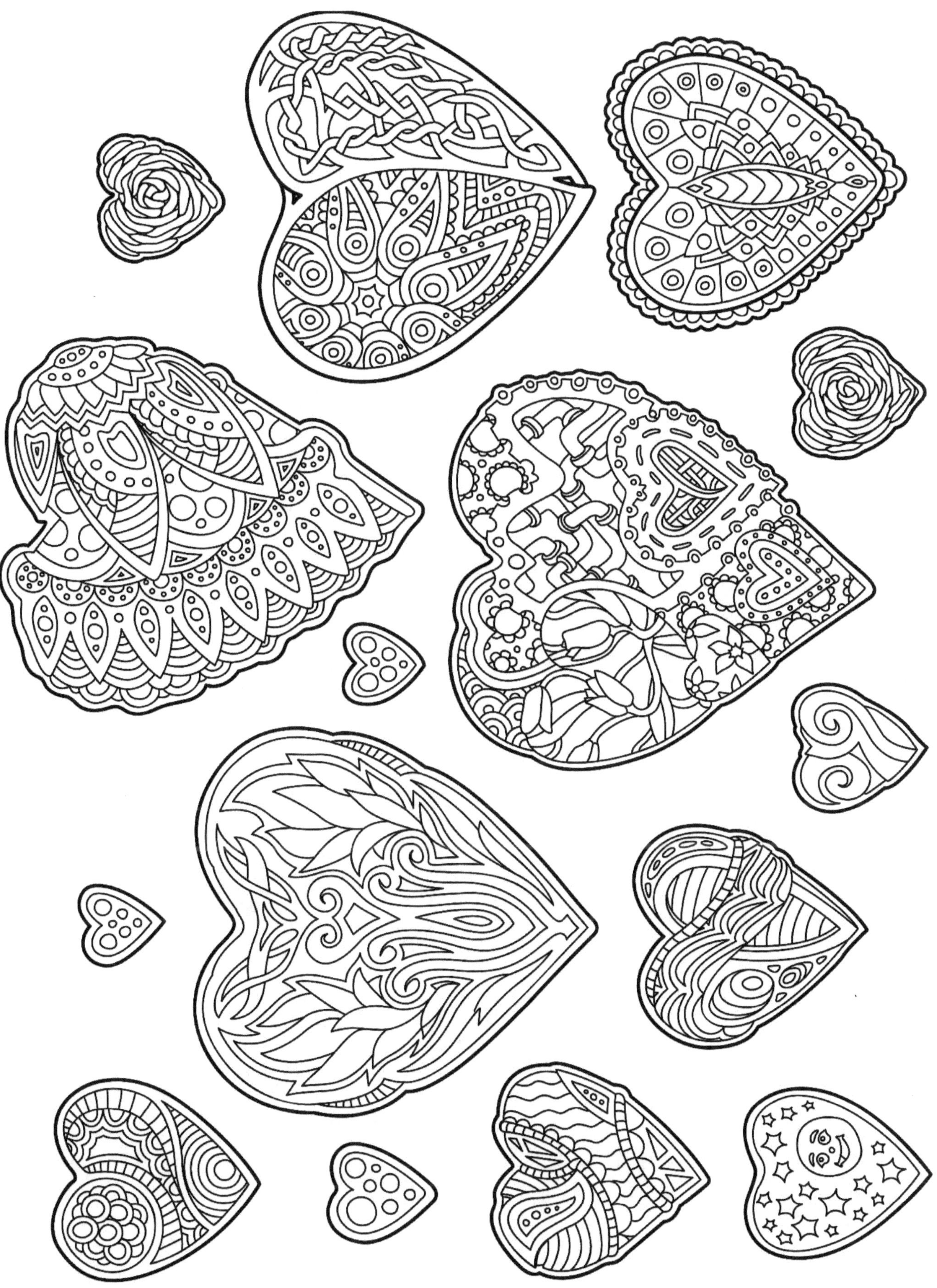

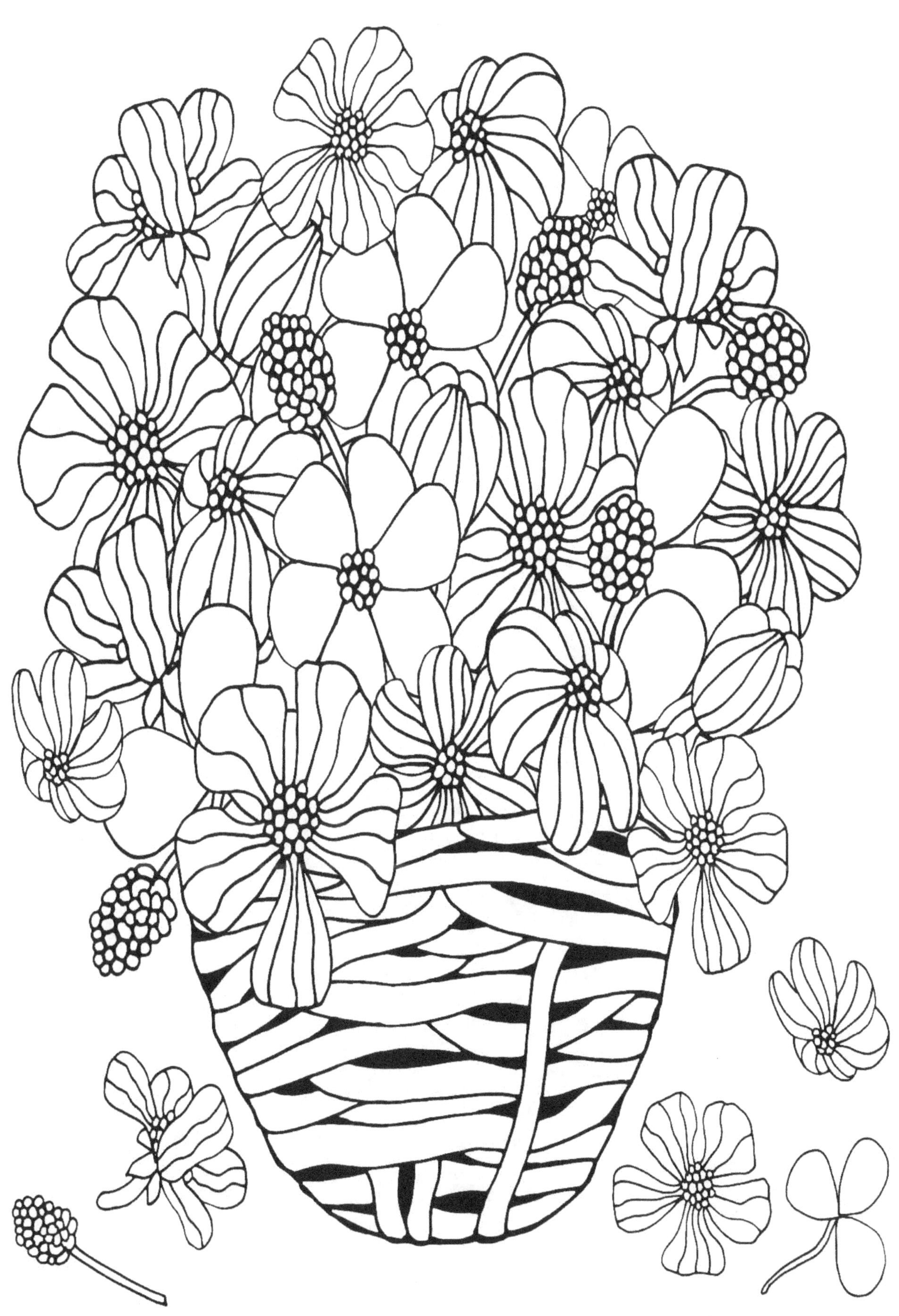

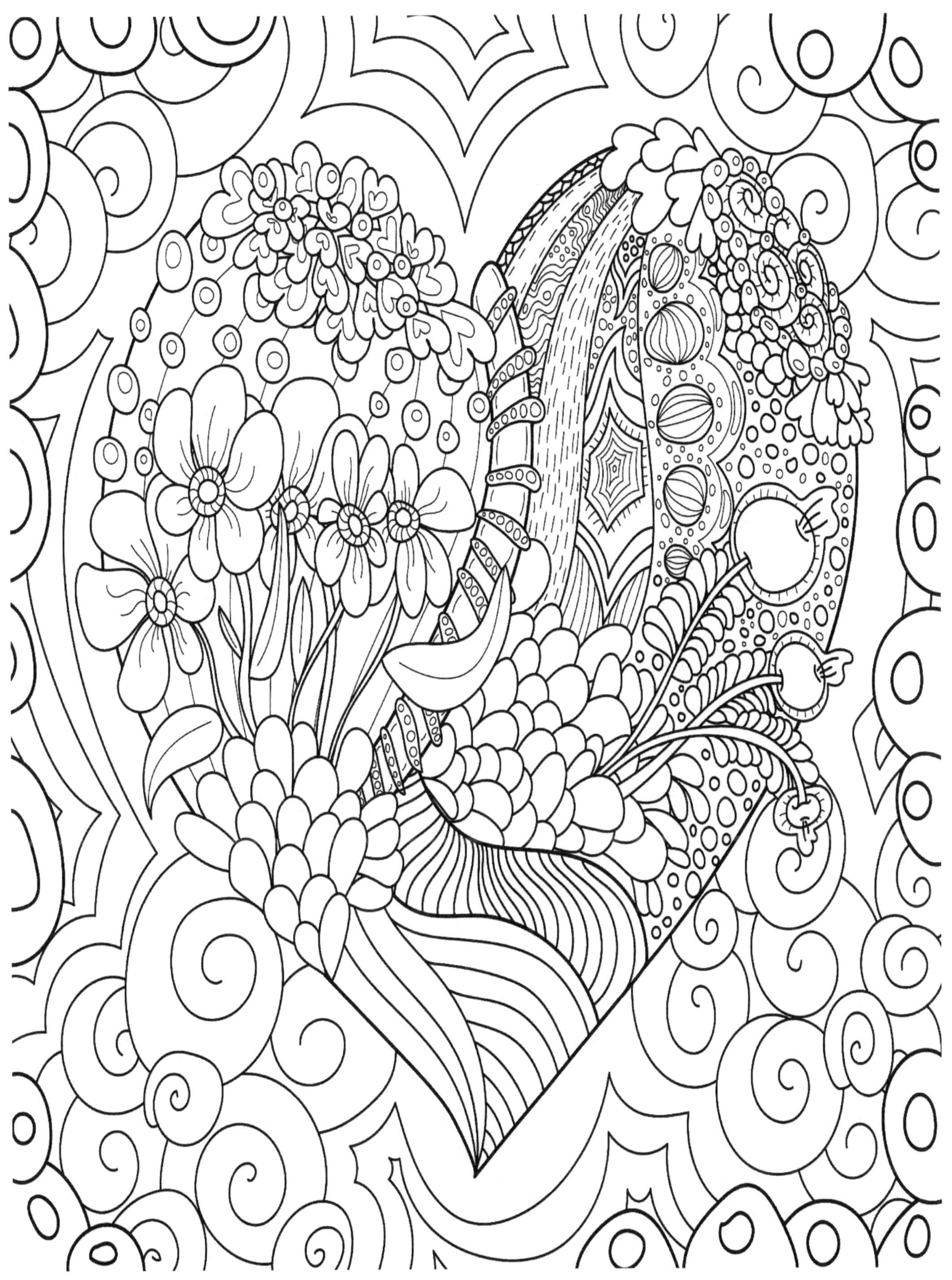

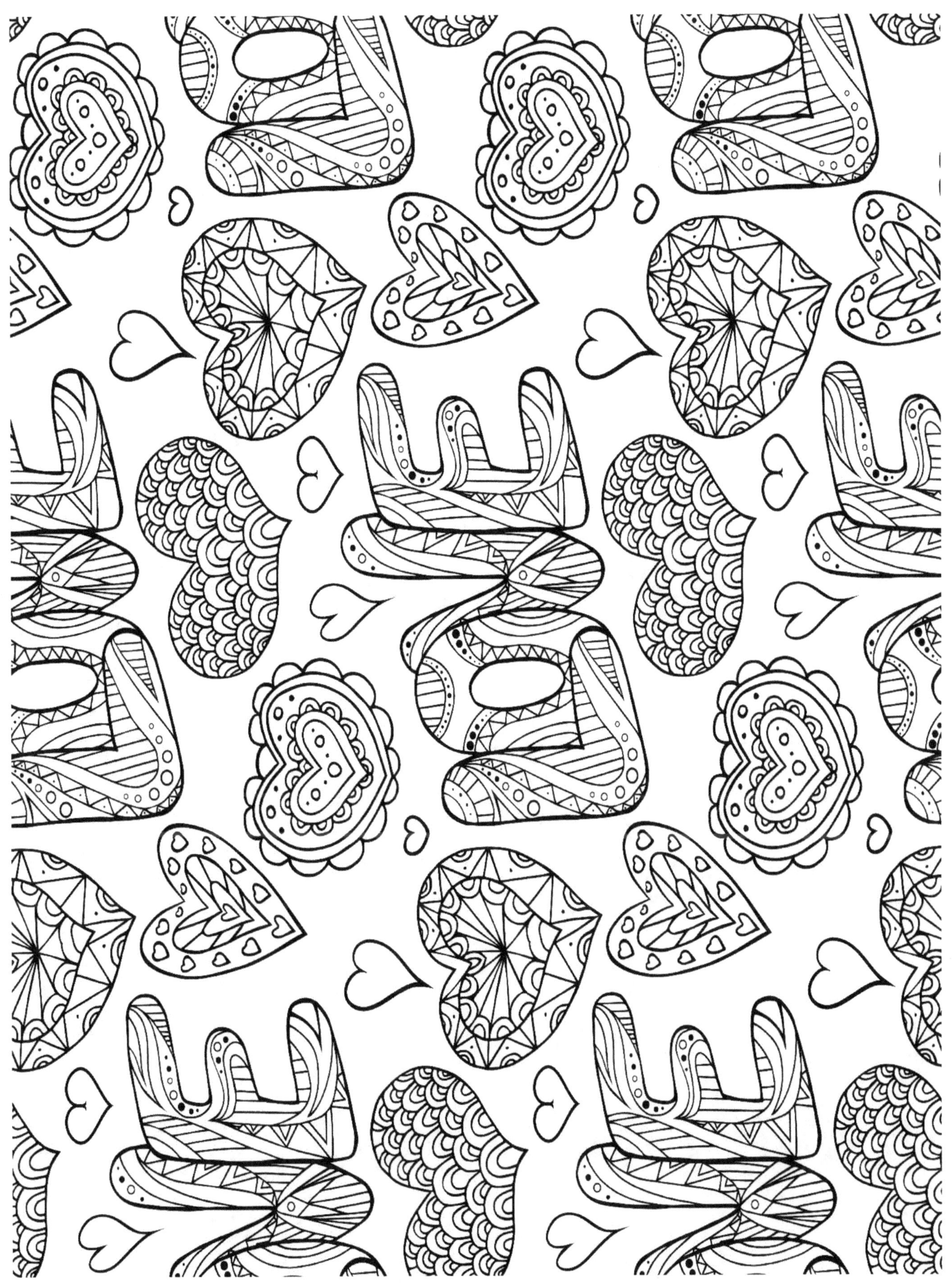

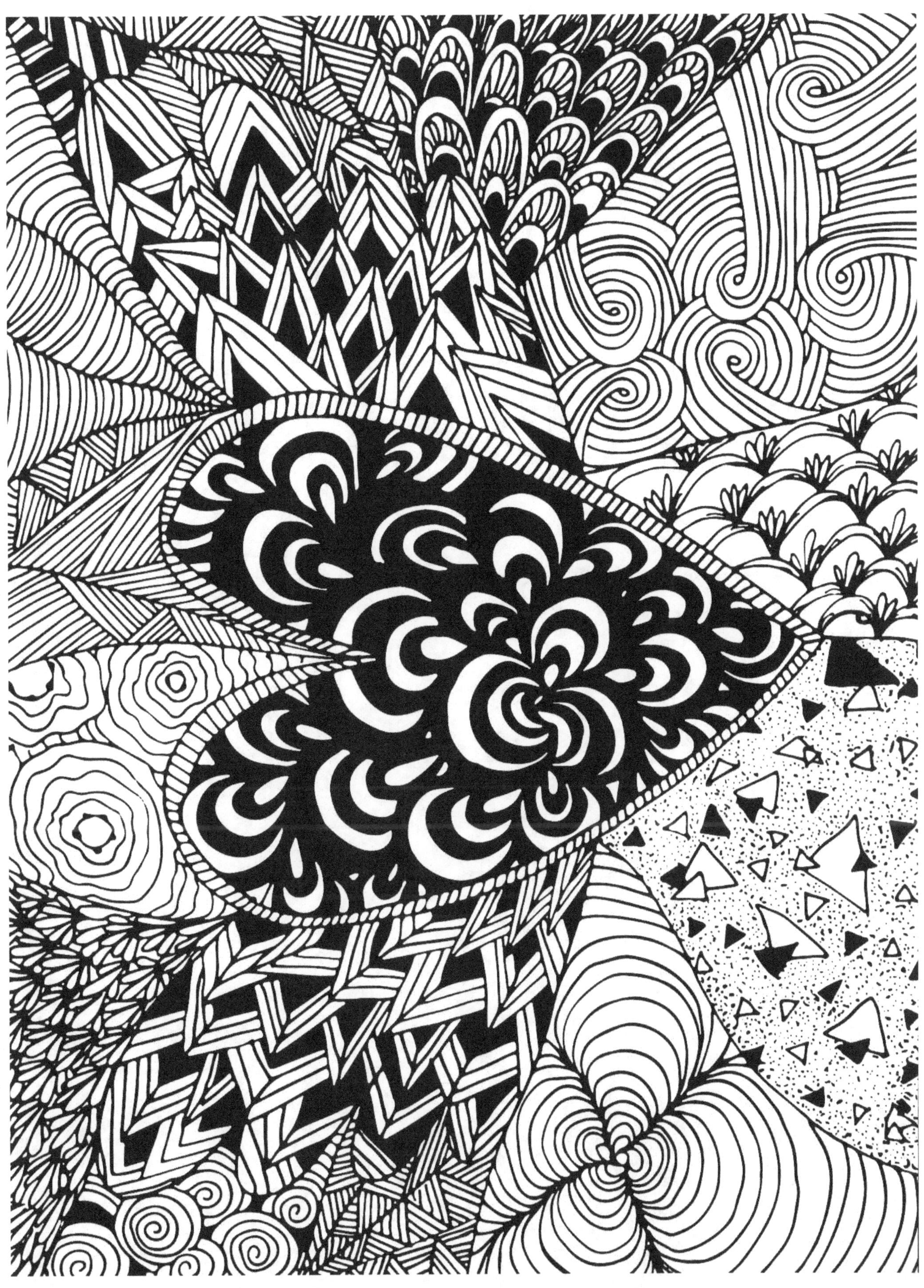

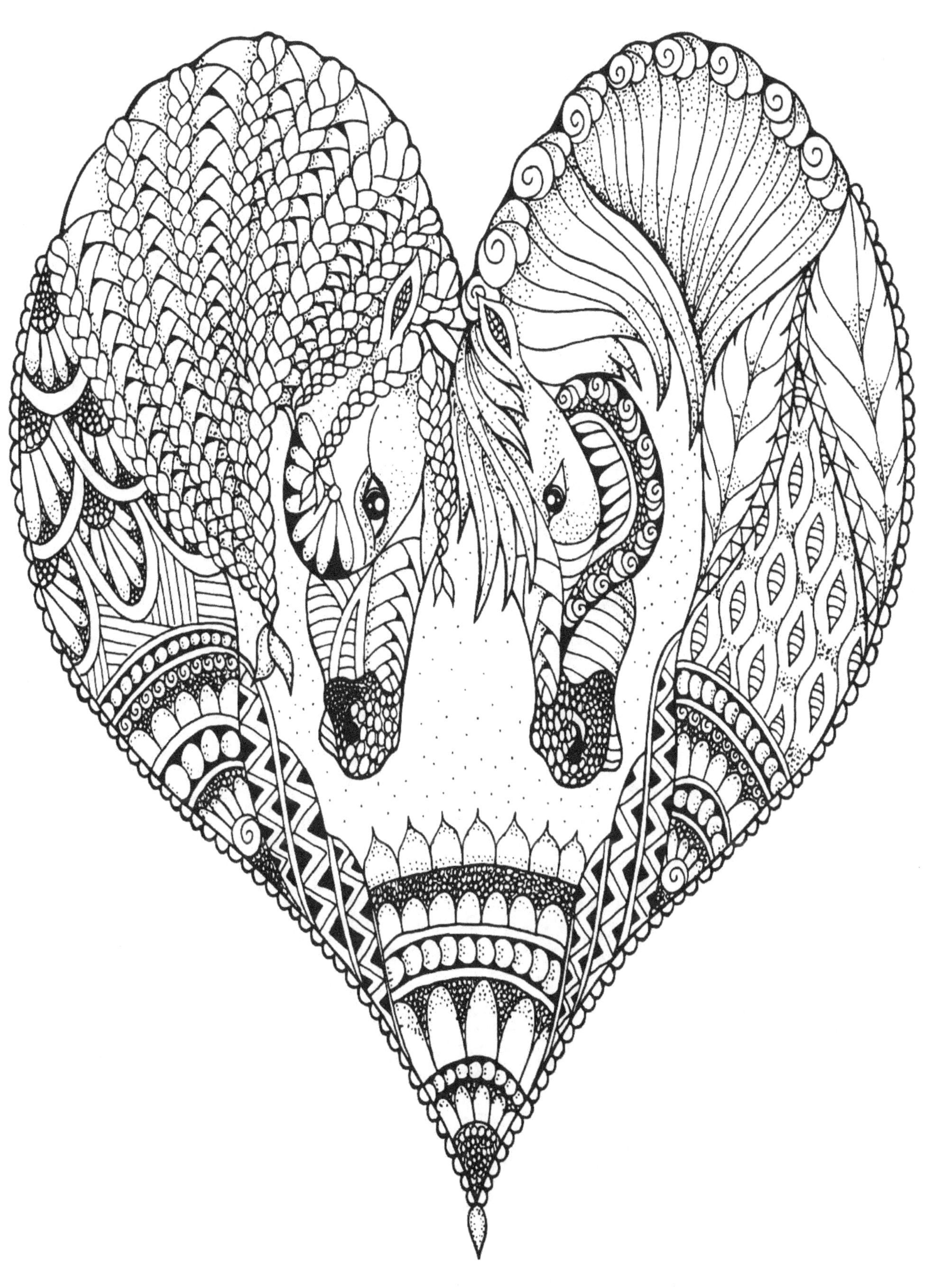

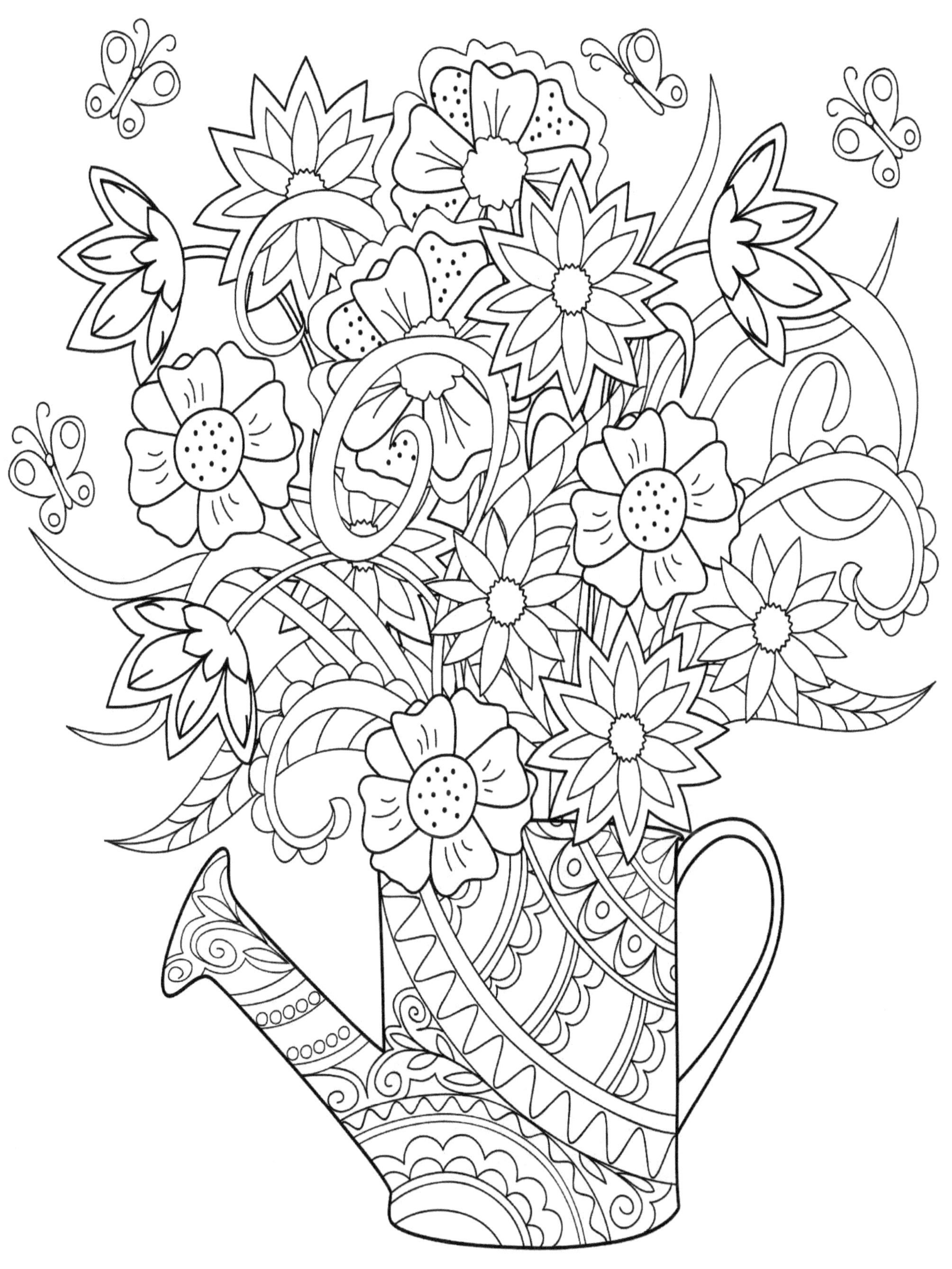

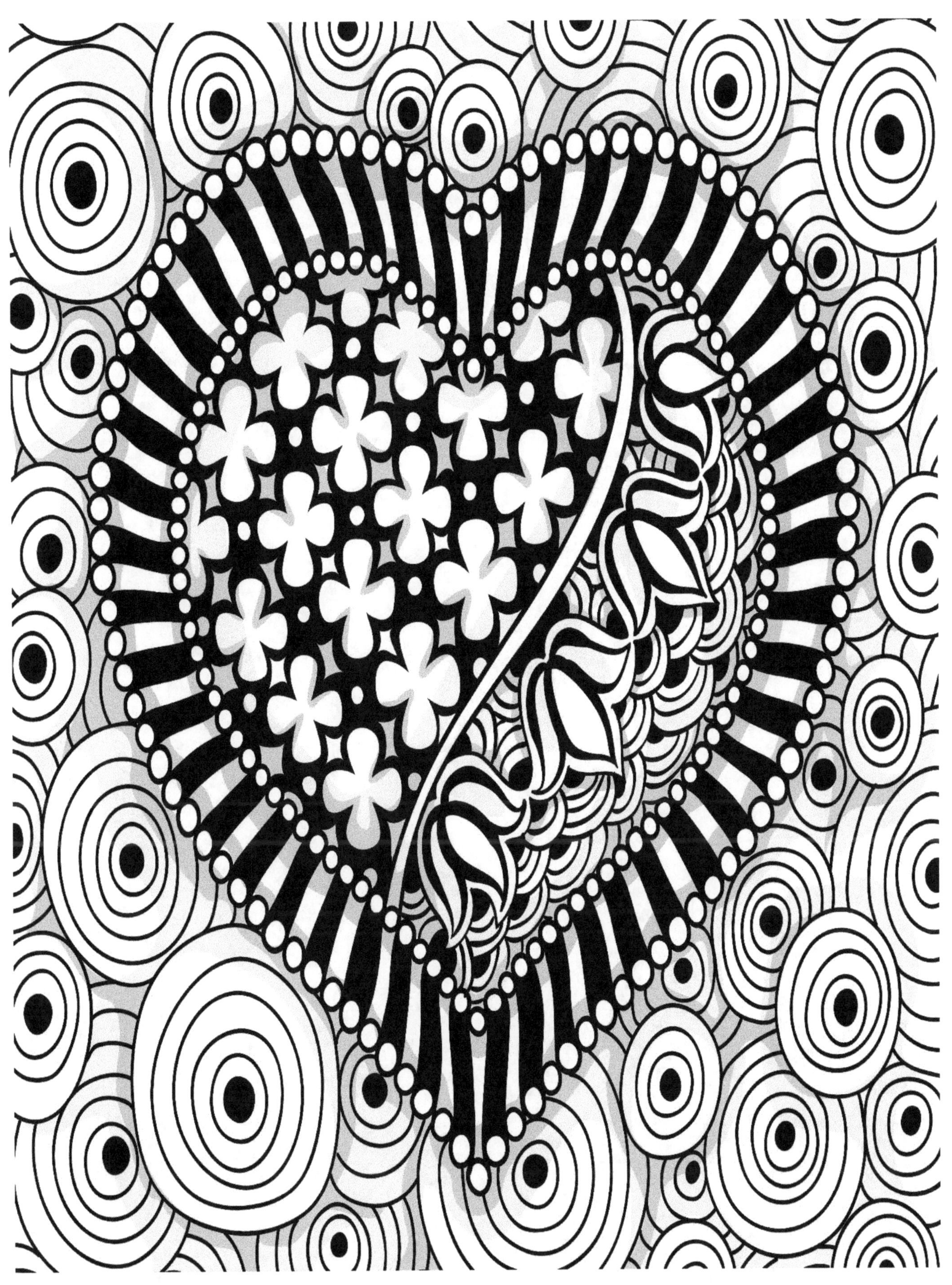

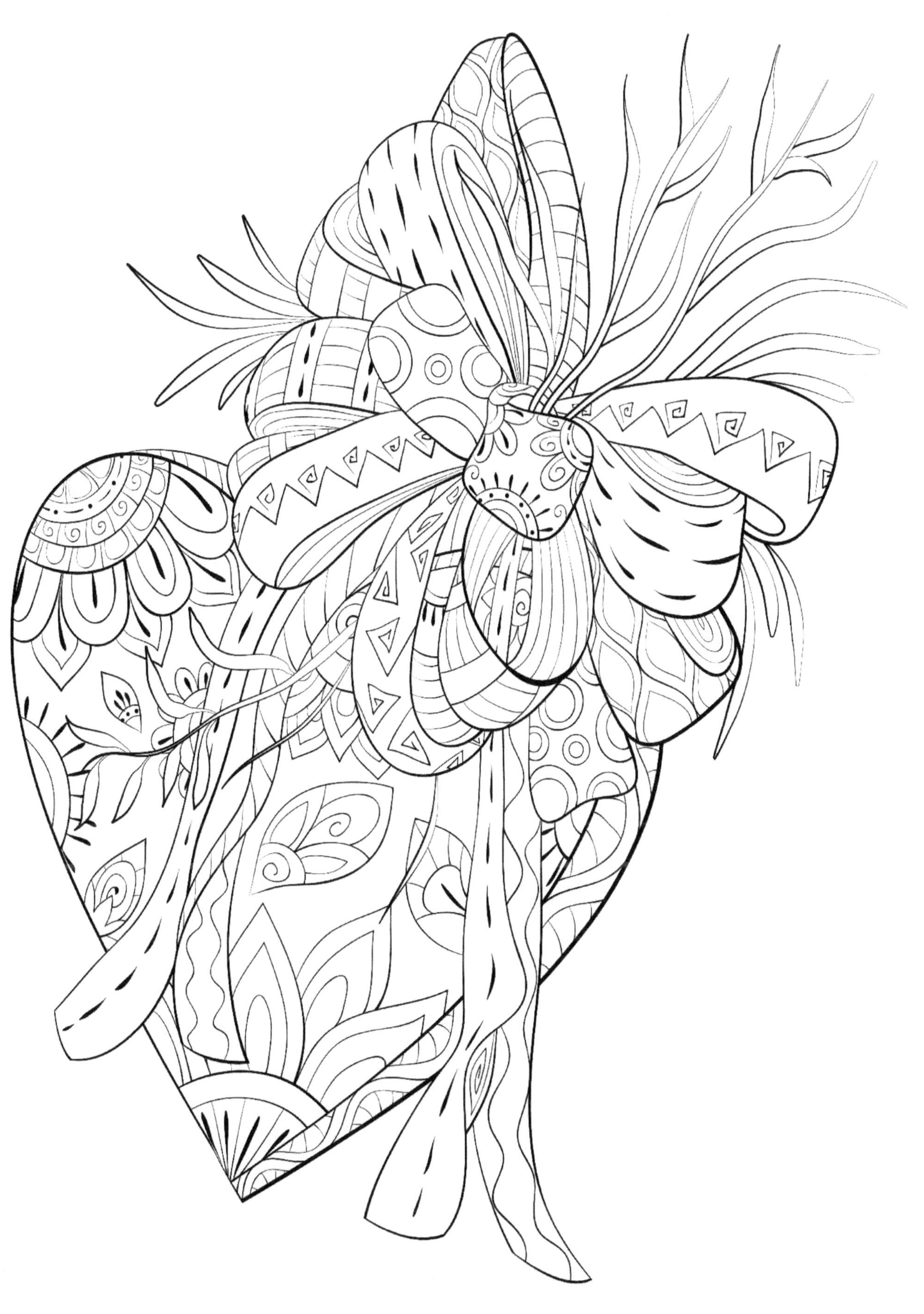

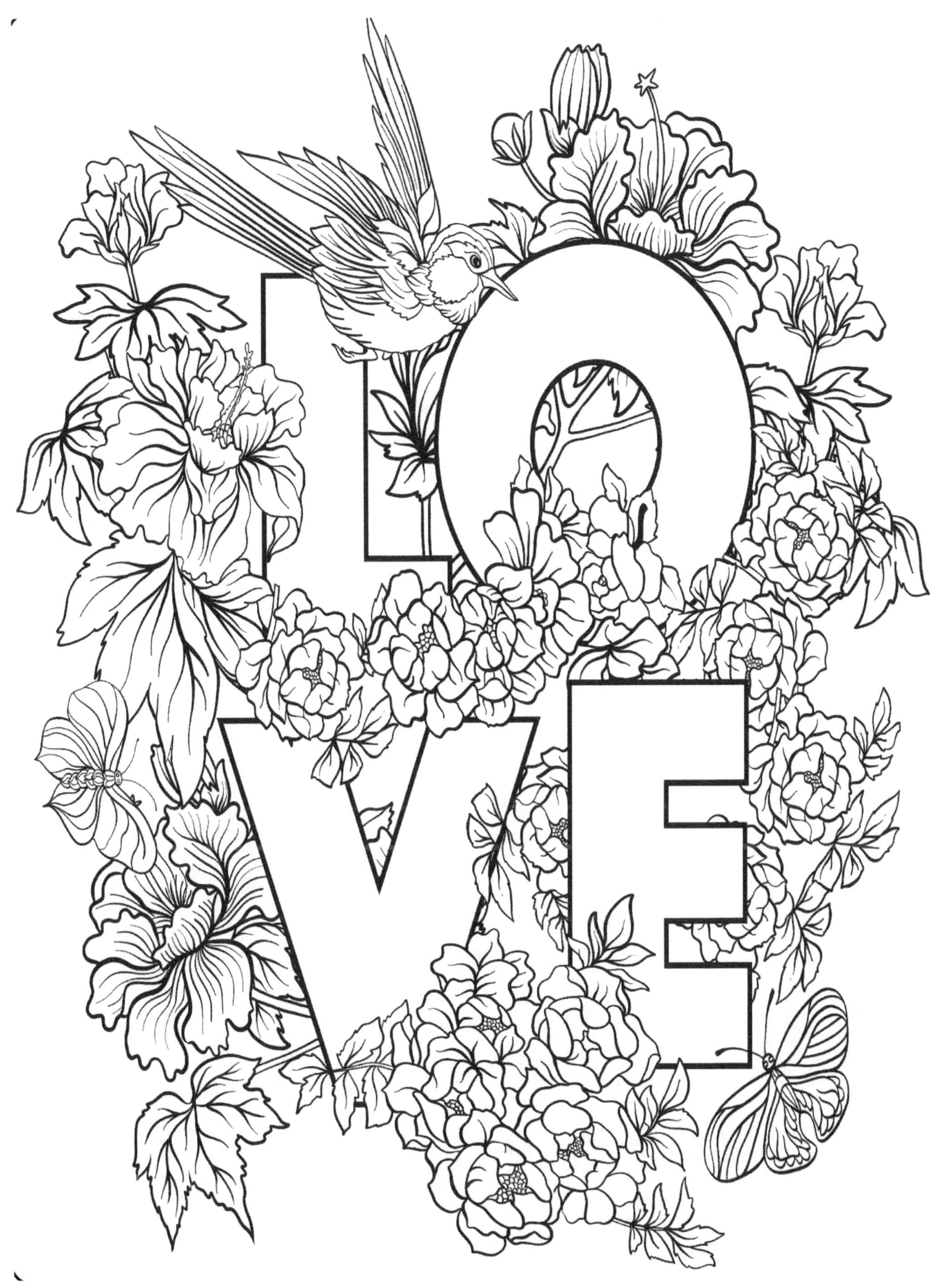
LOVE

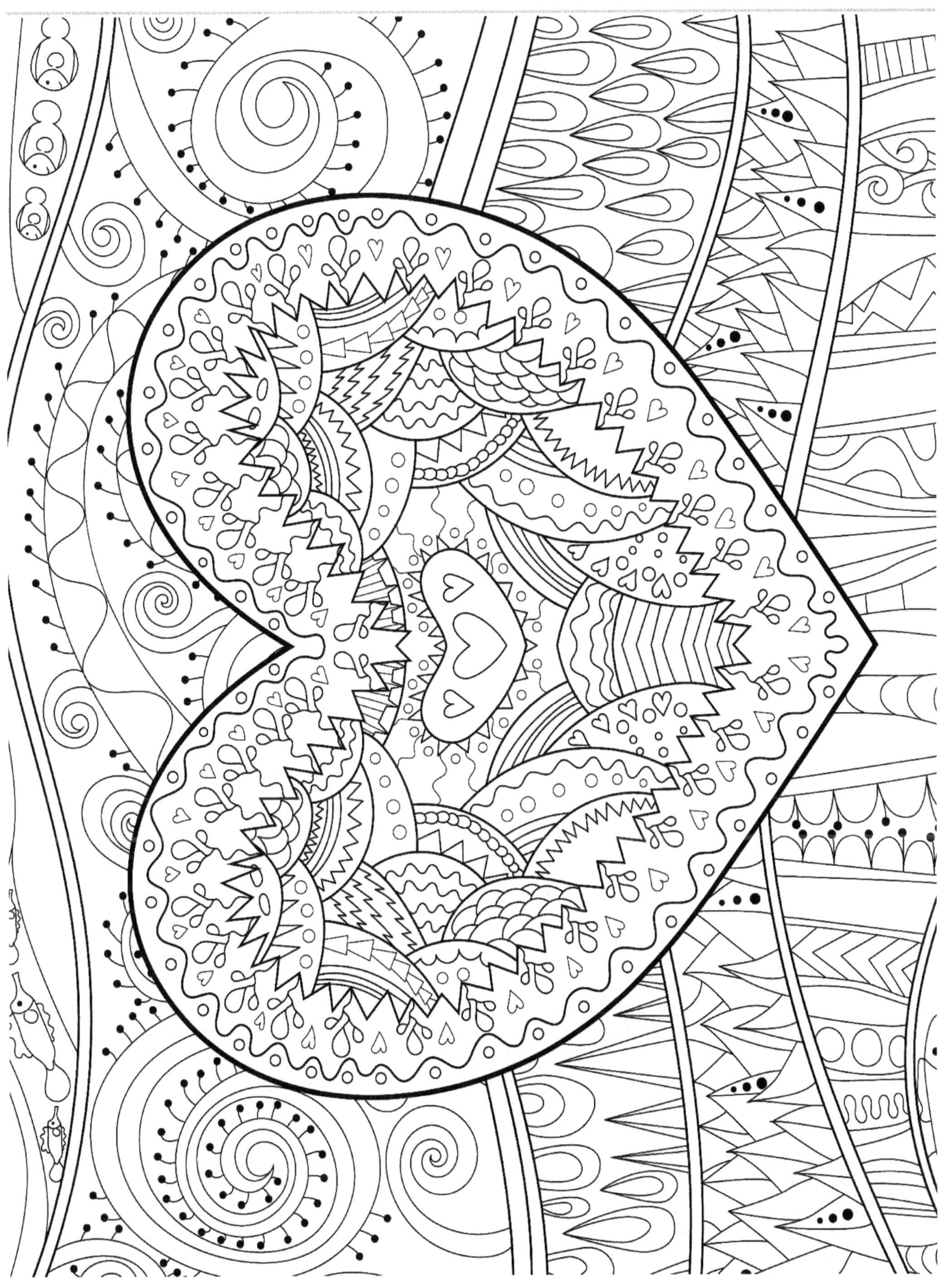

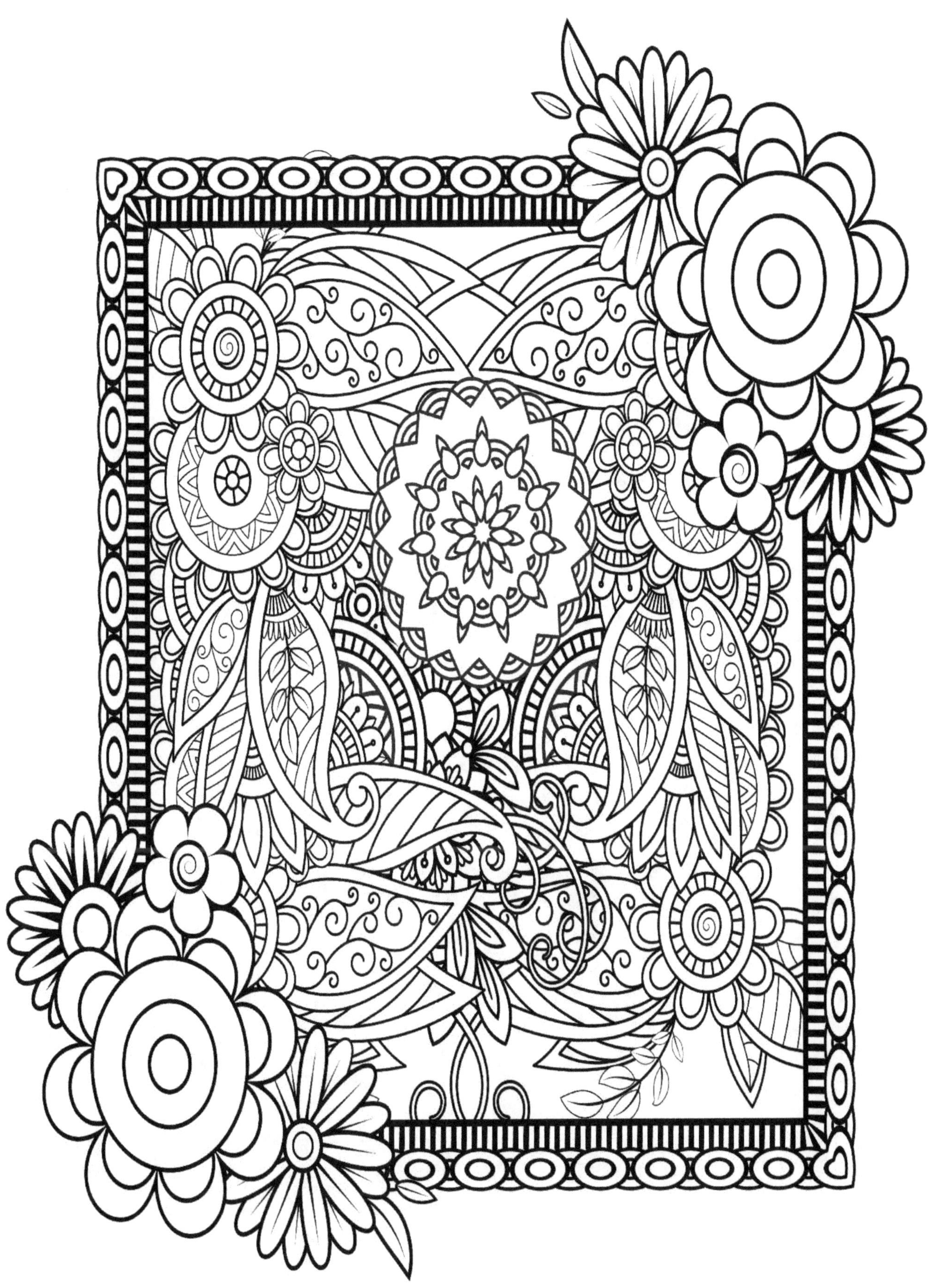

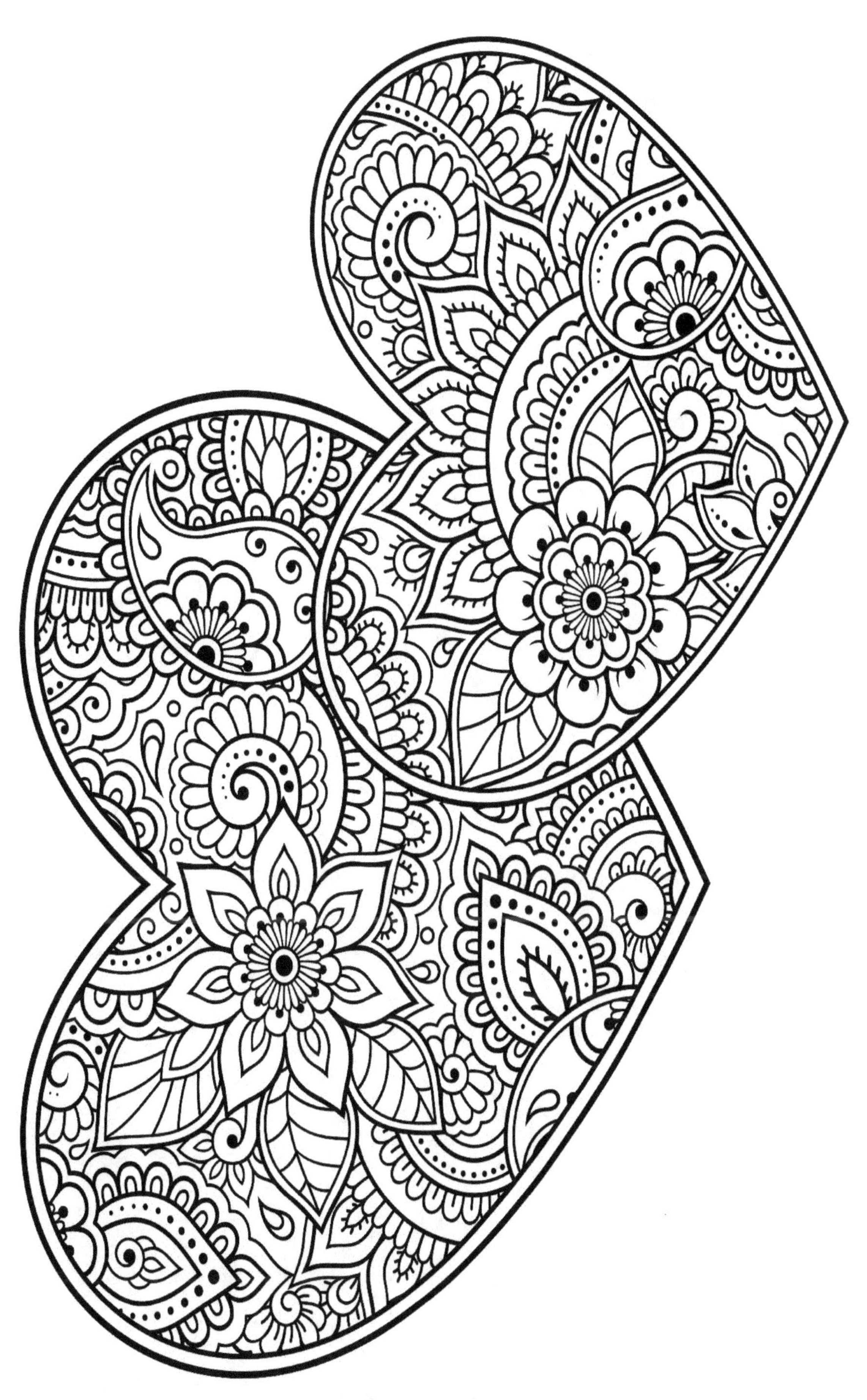

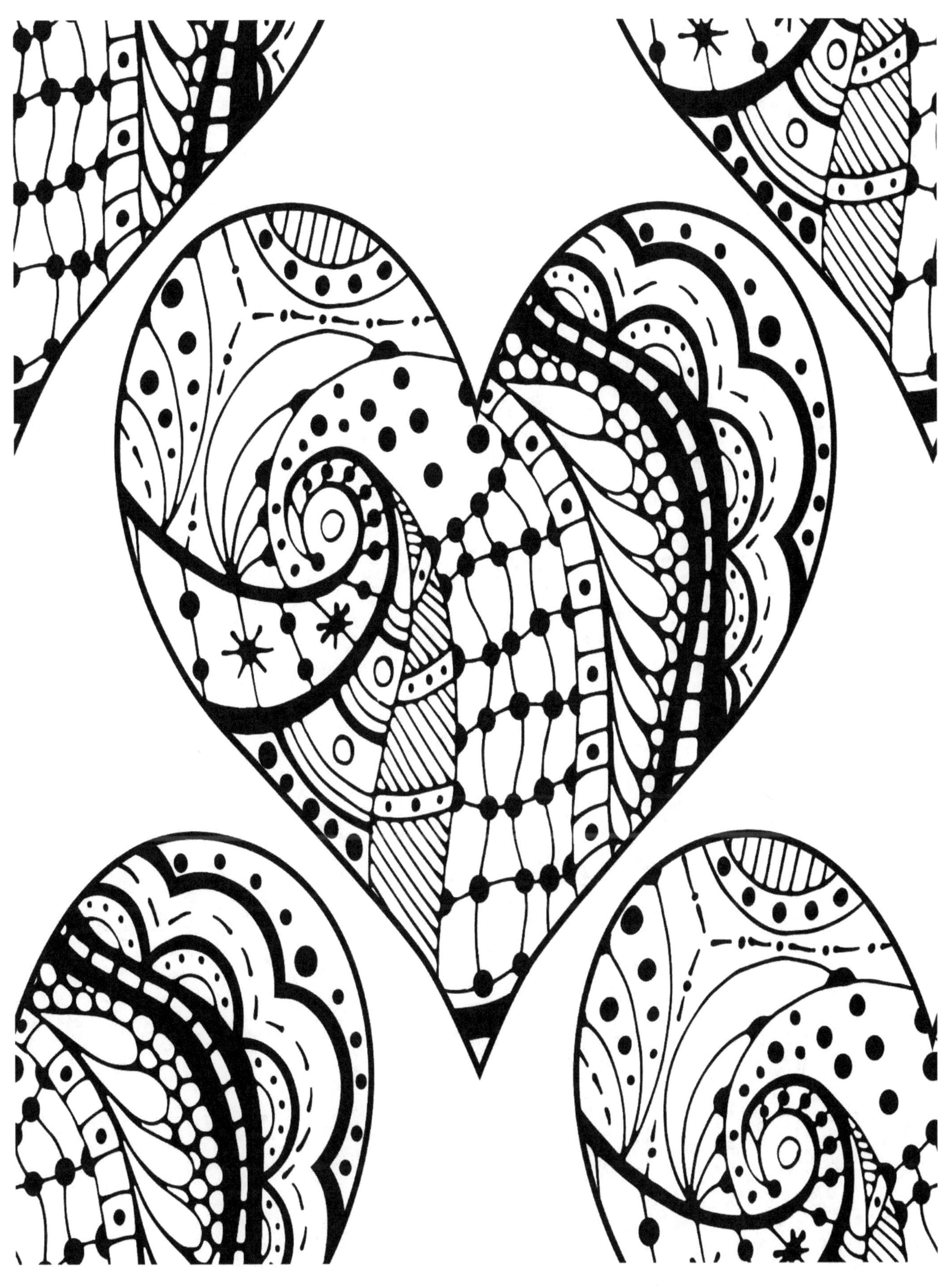

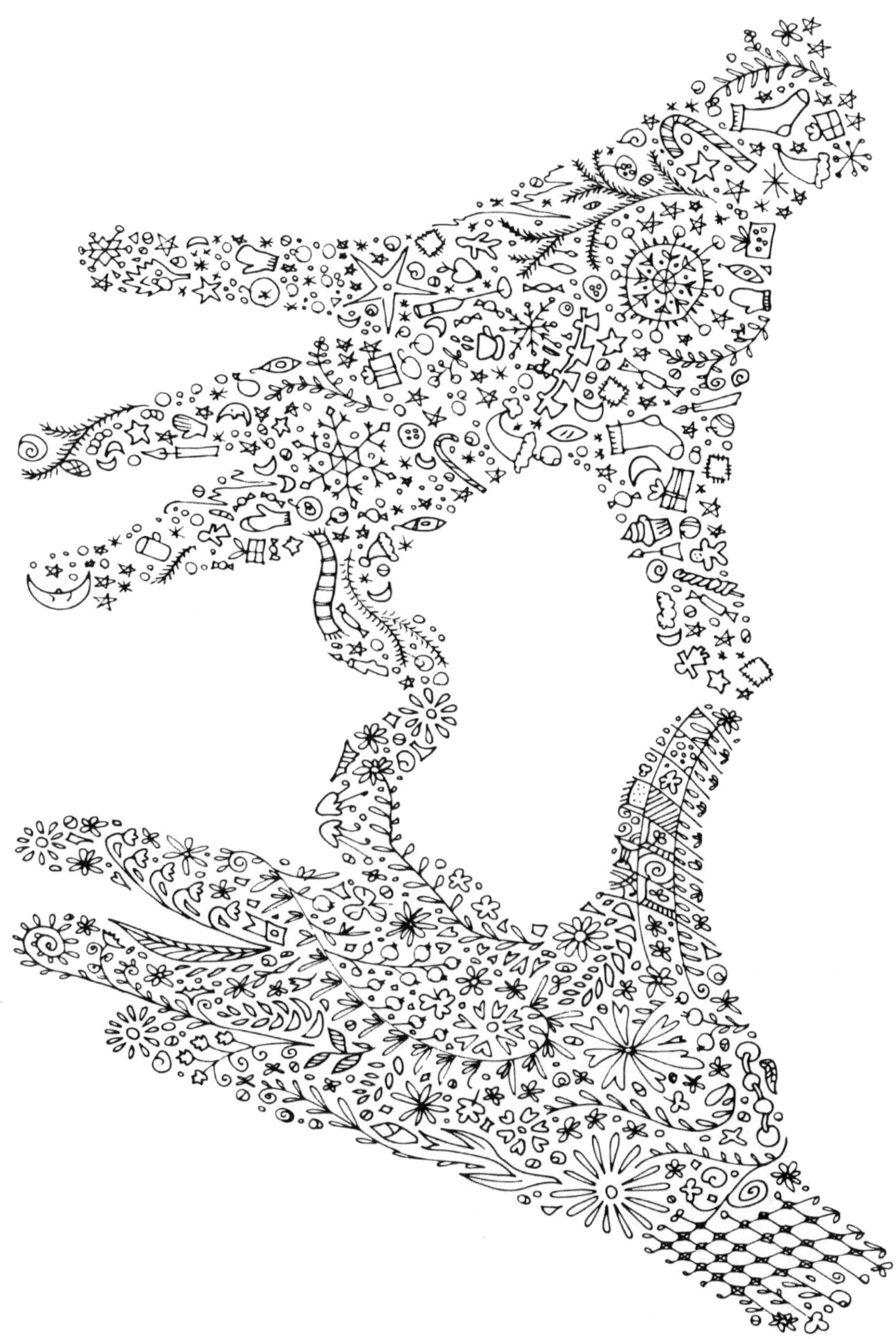

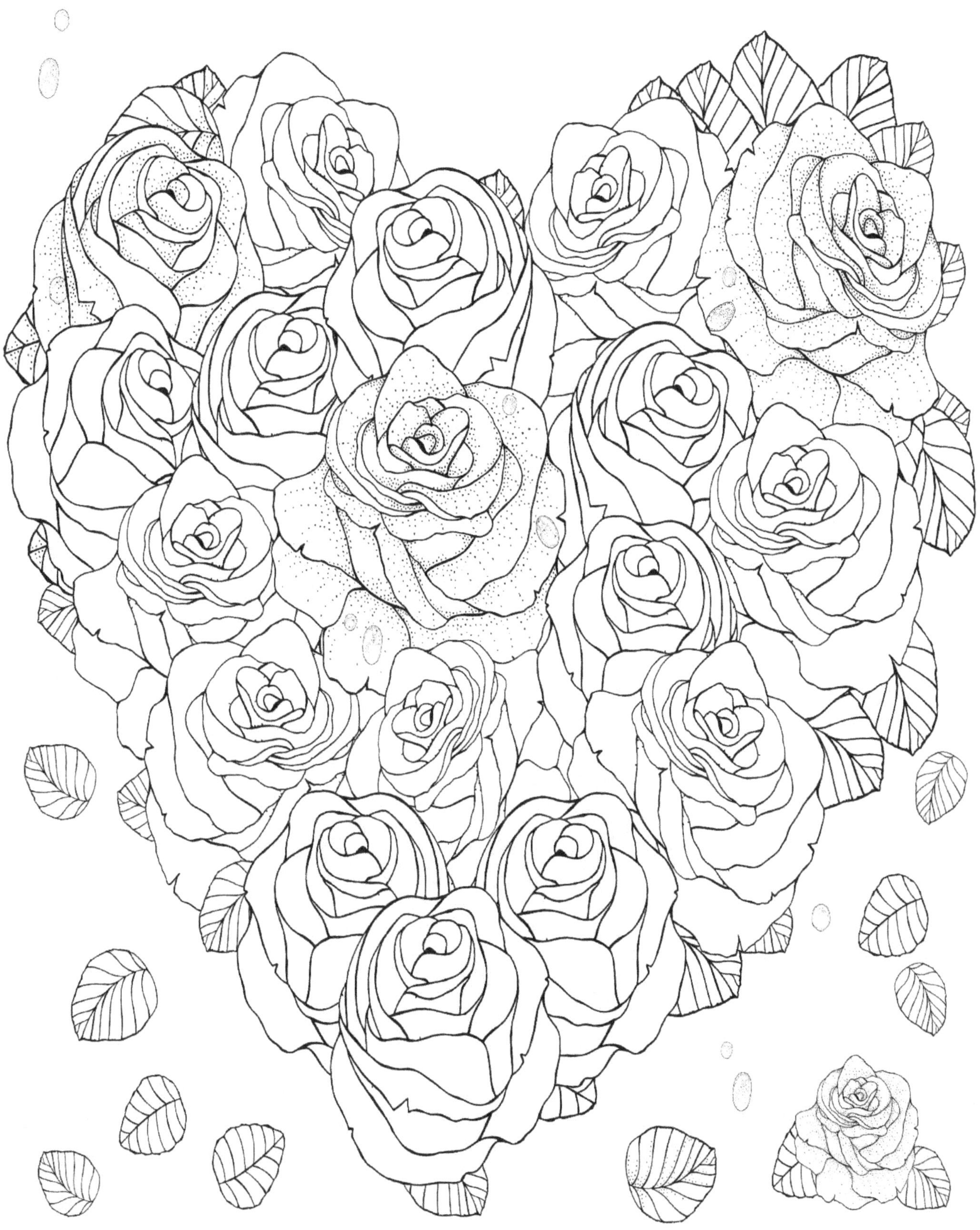

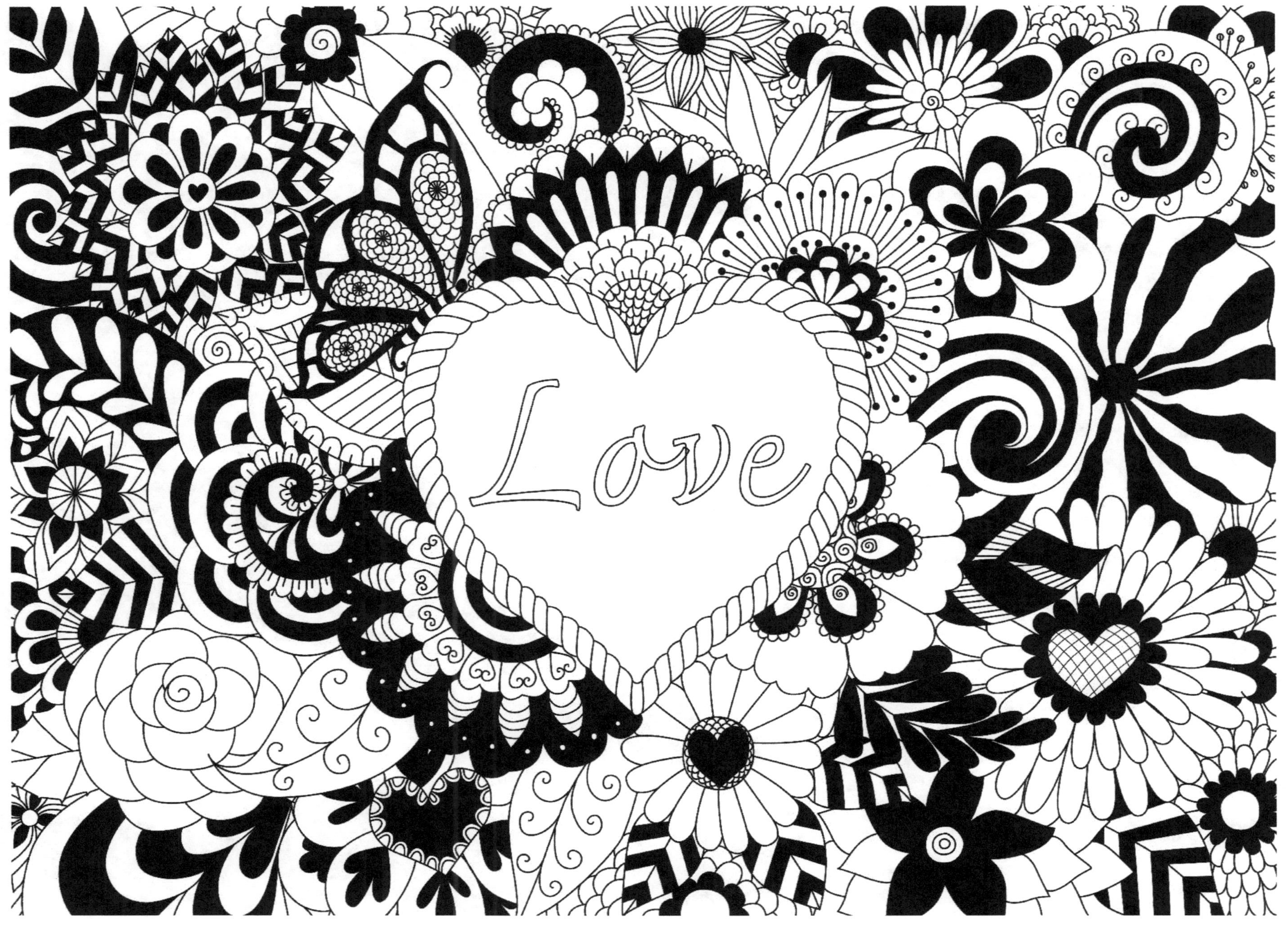
Love

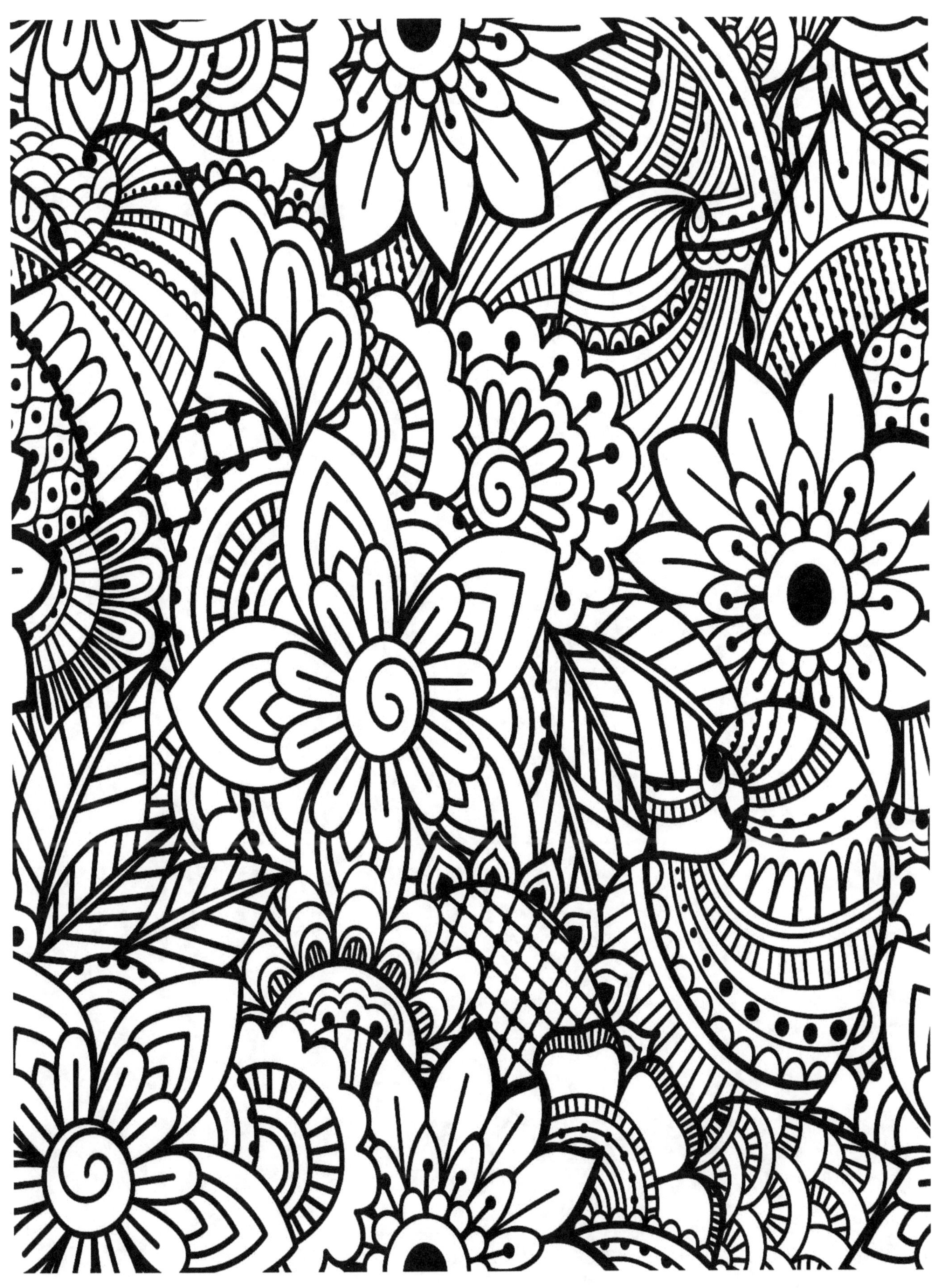

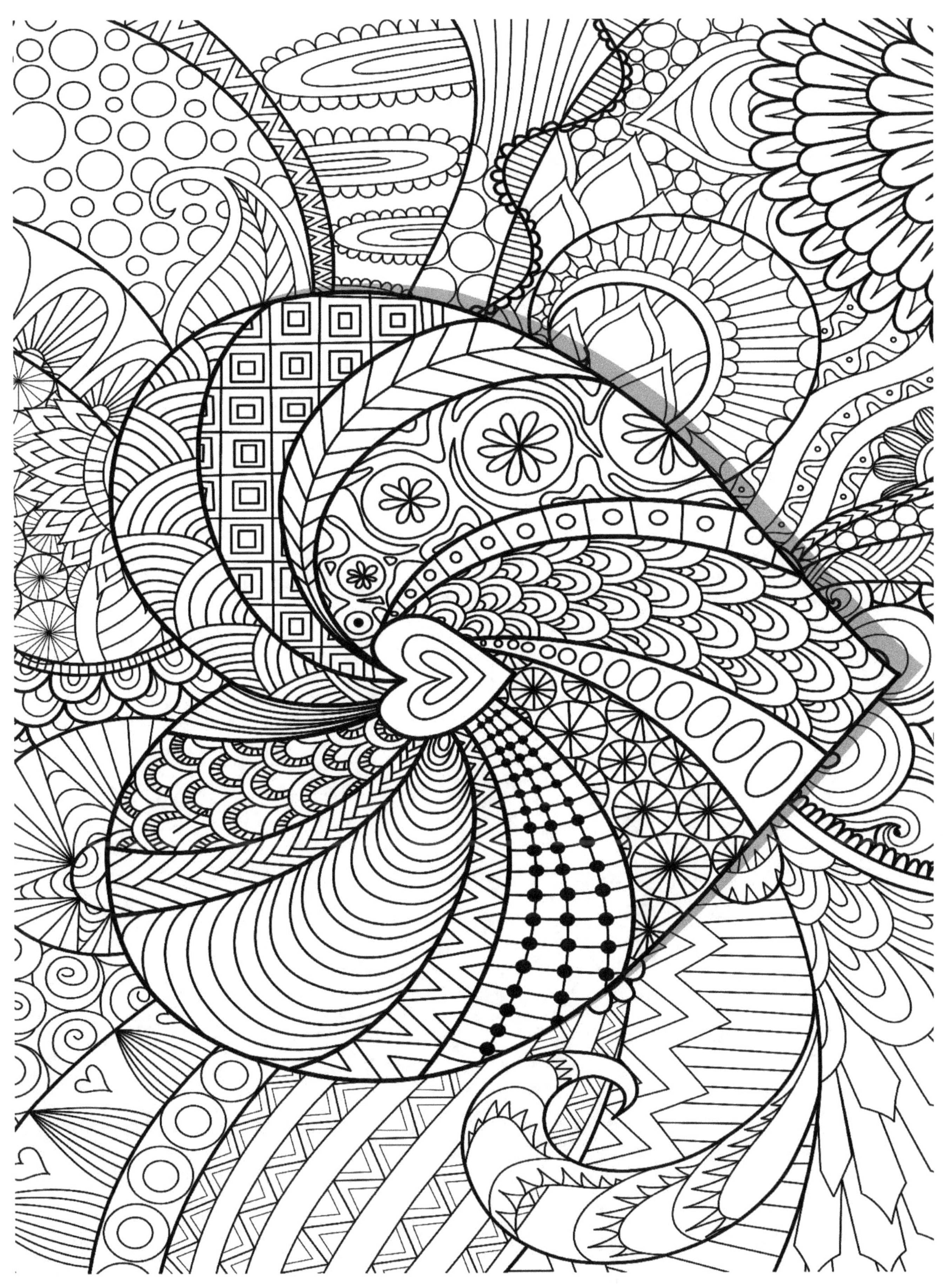

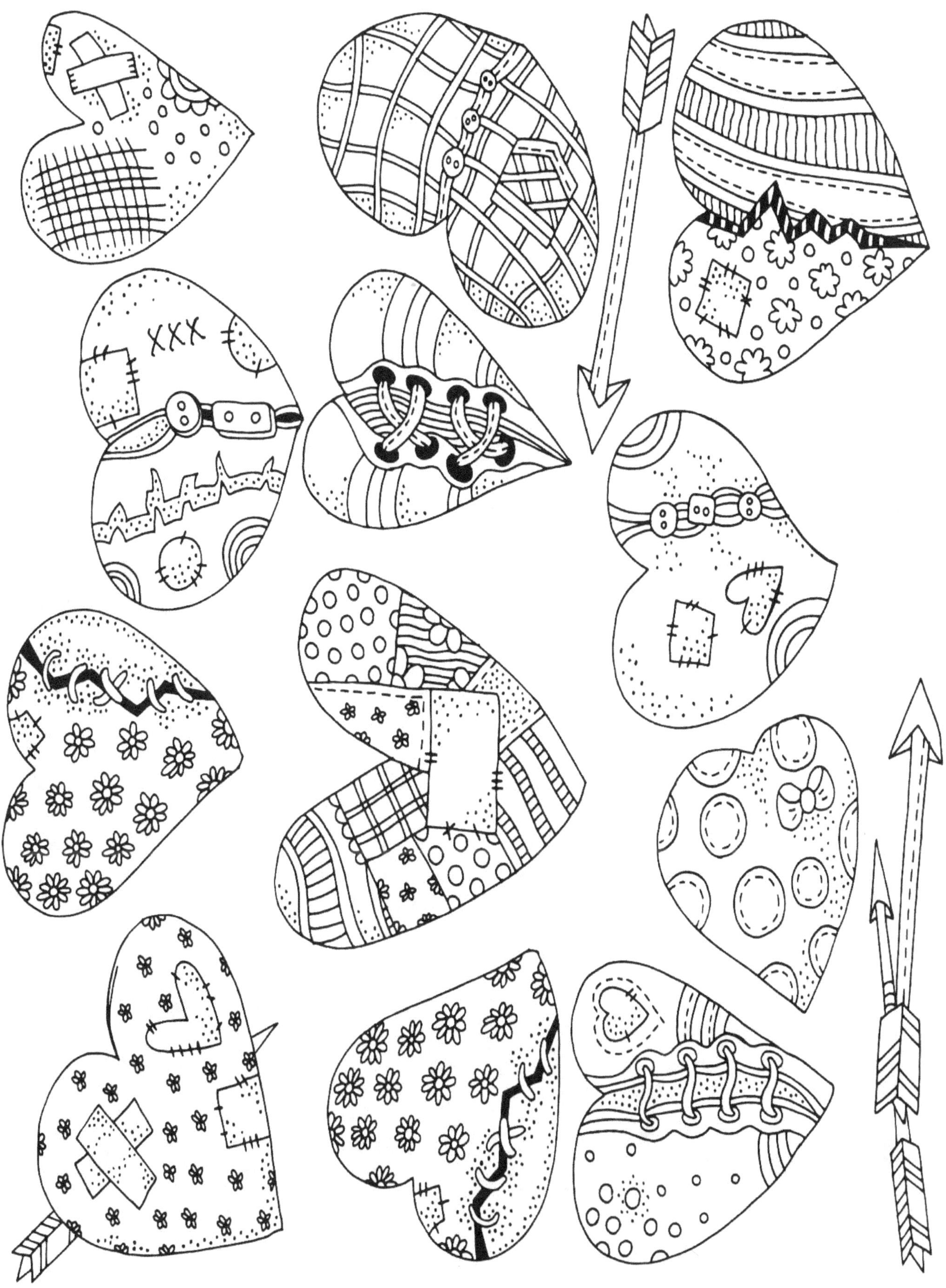

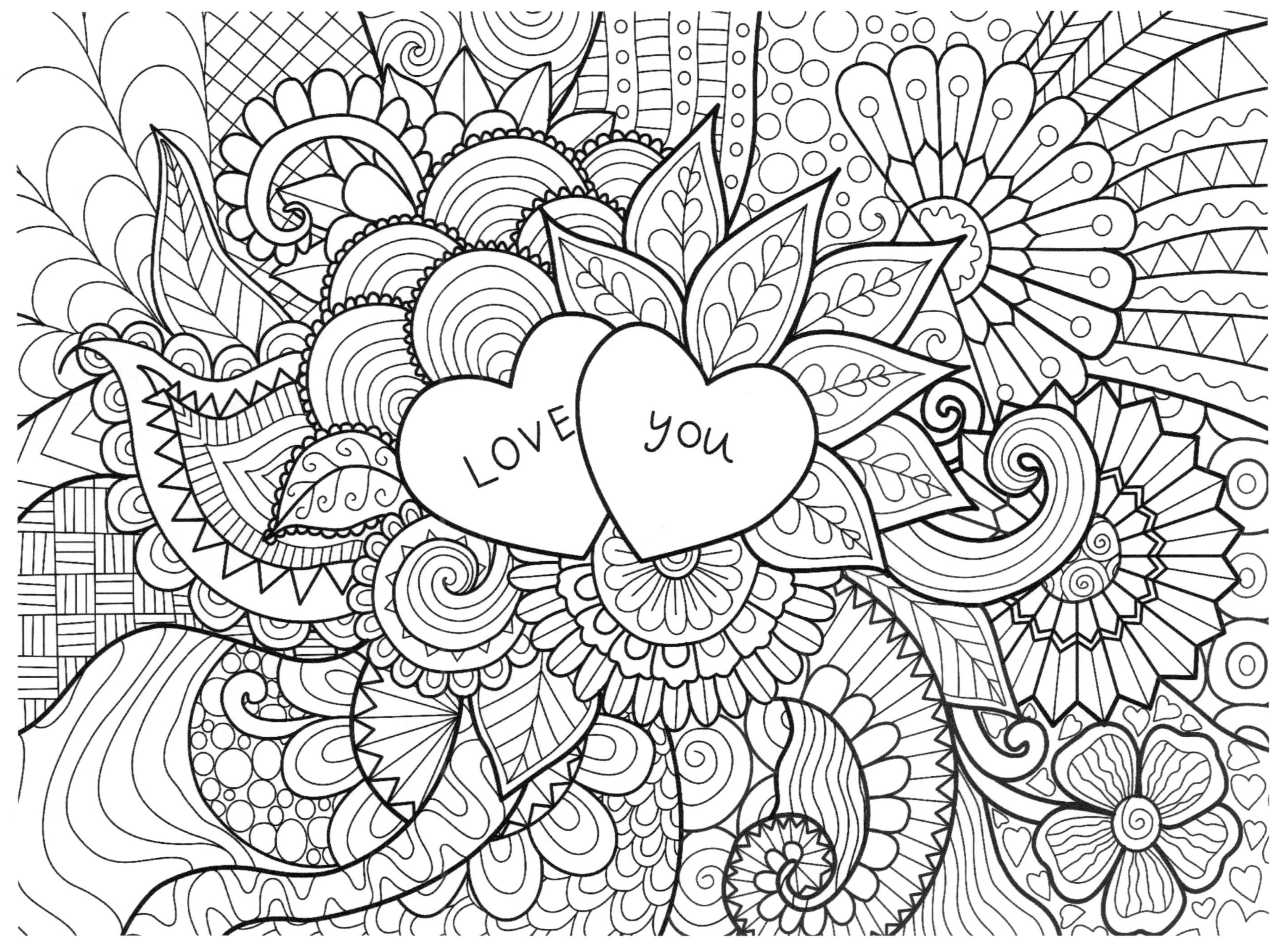
LOVE you

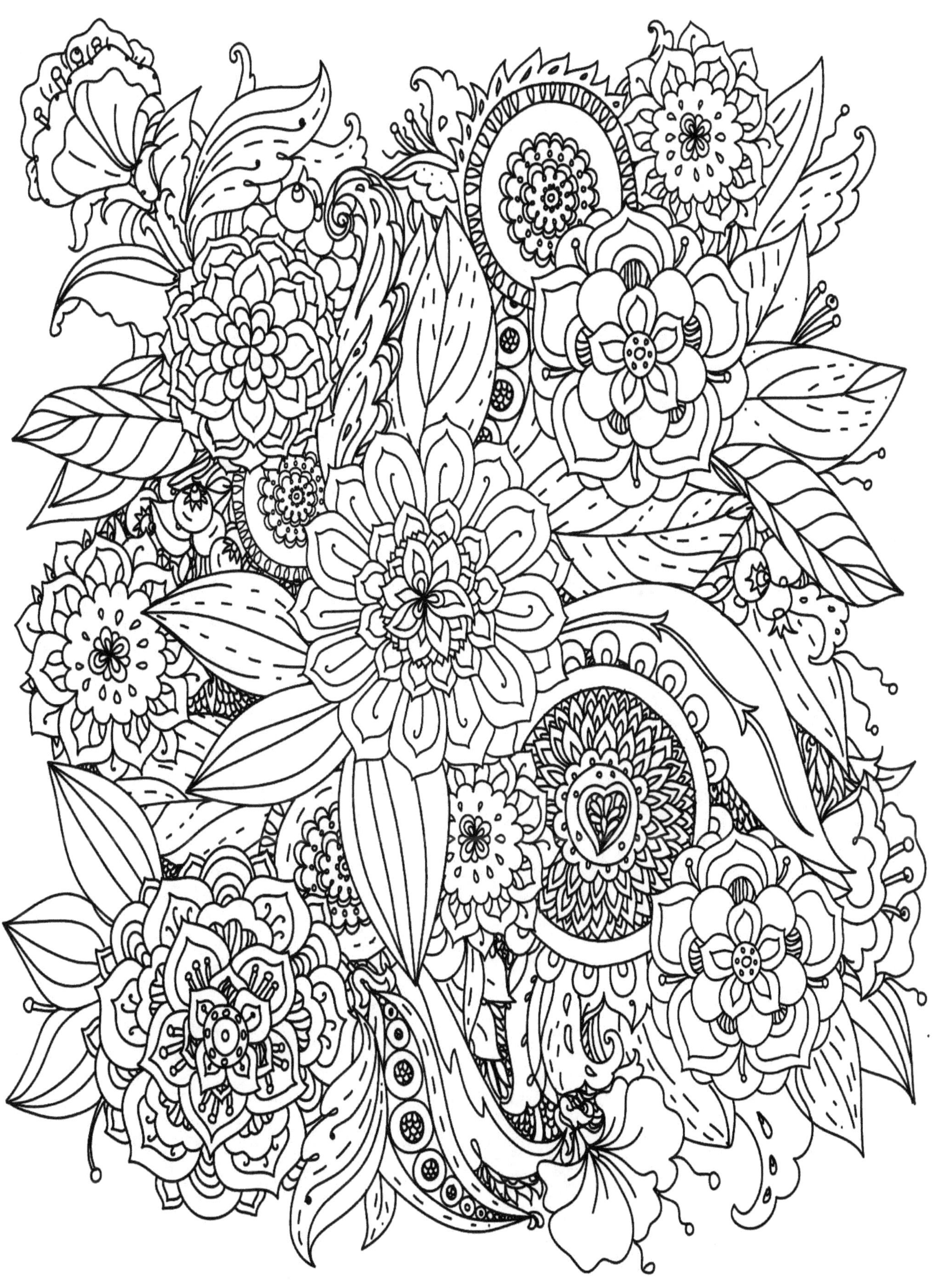

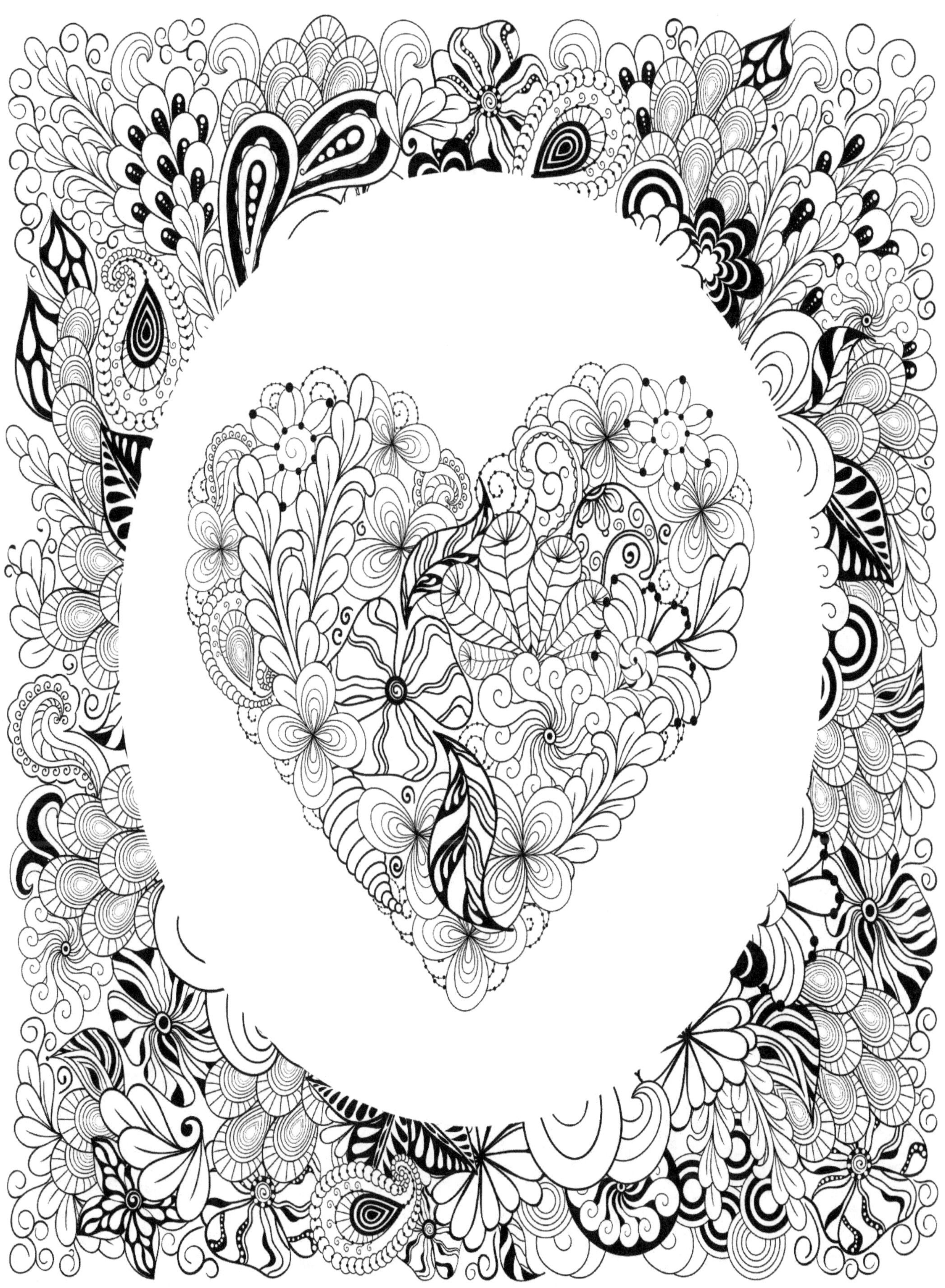

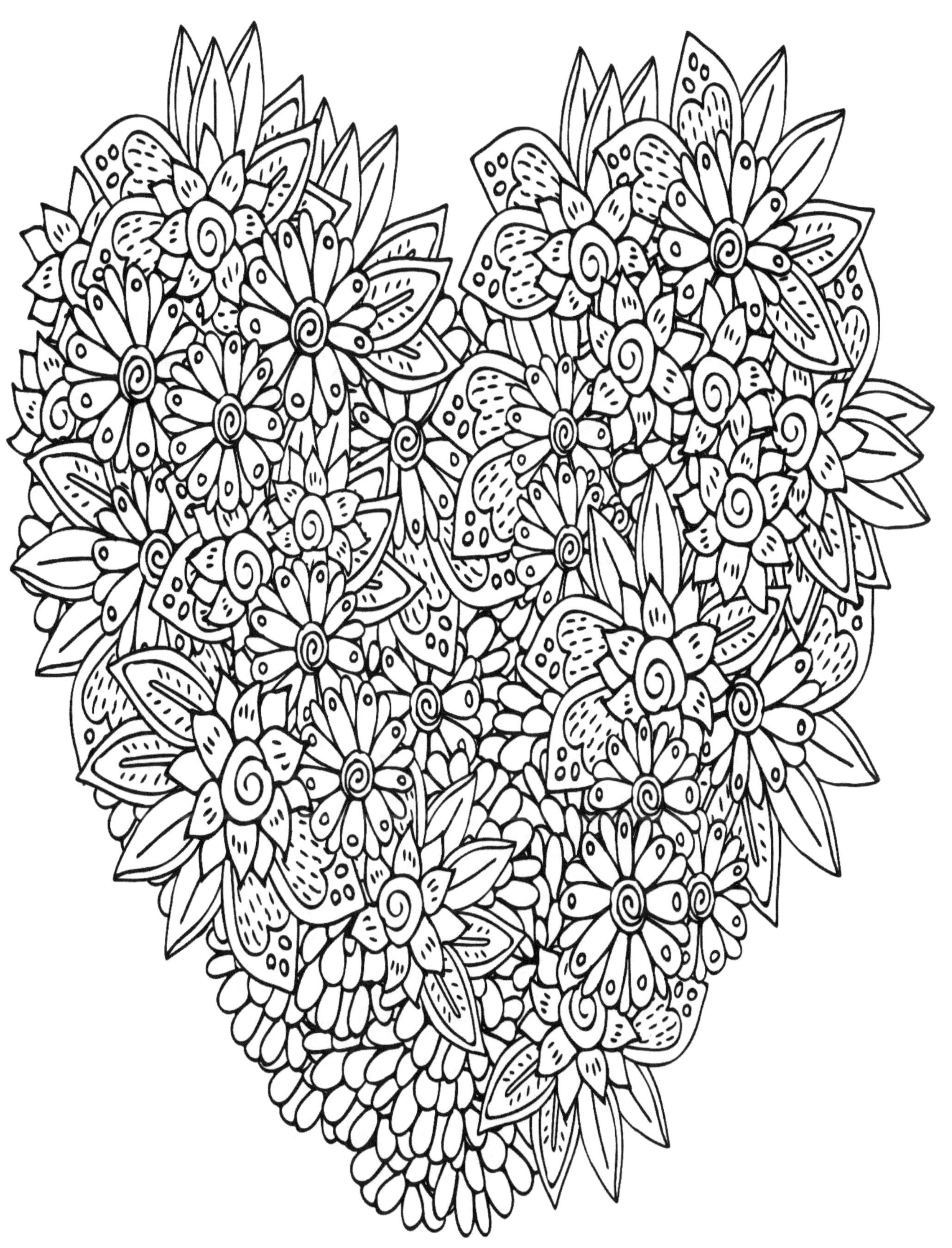

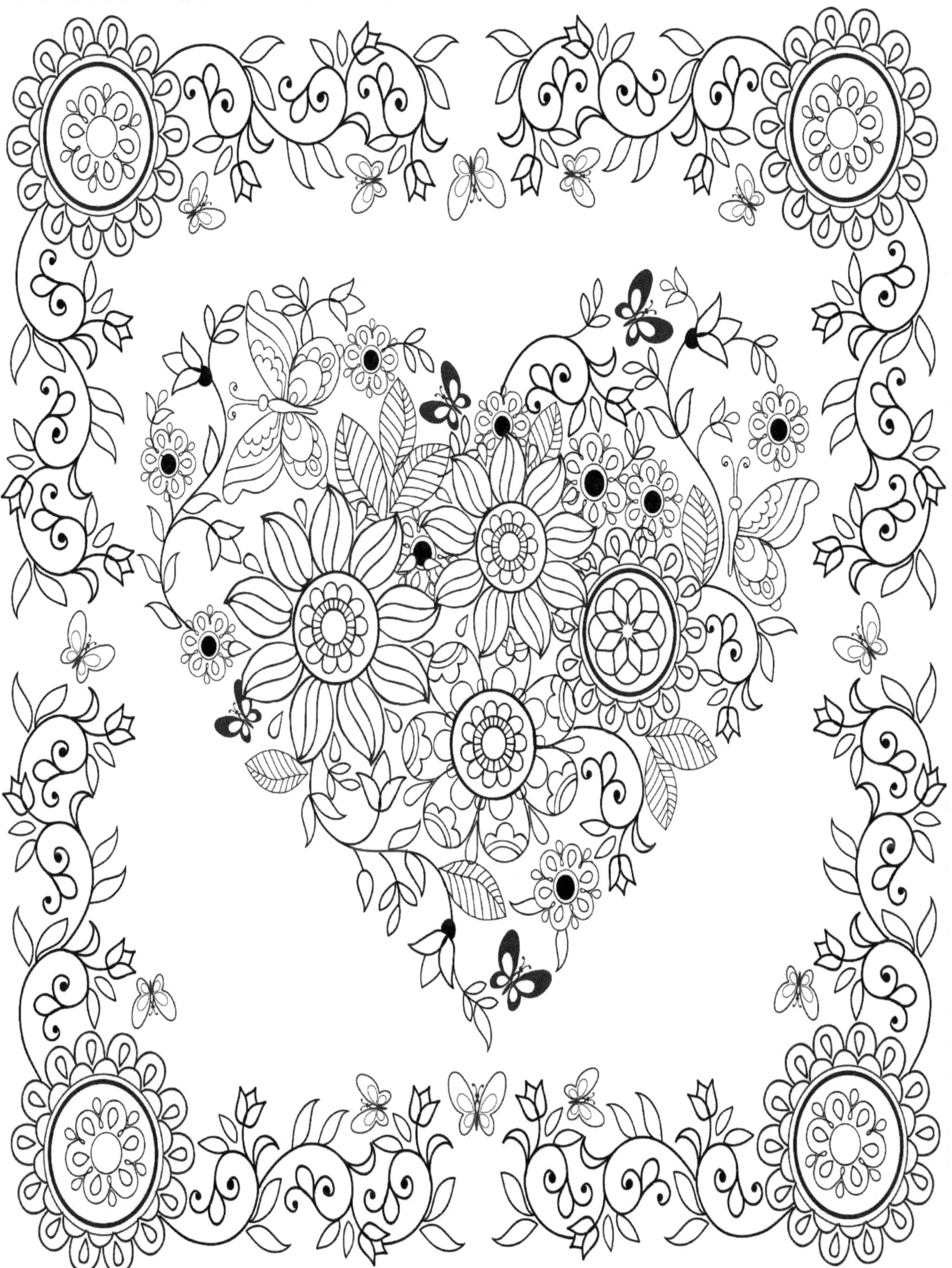

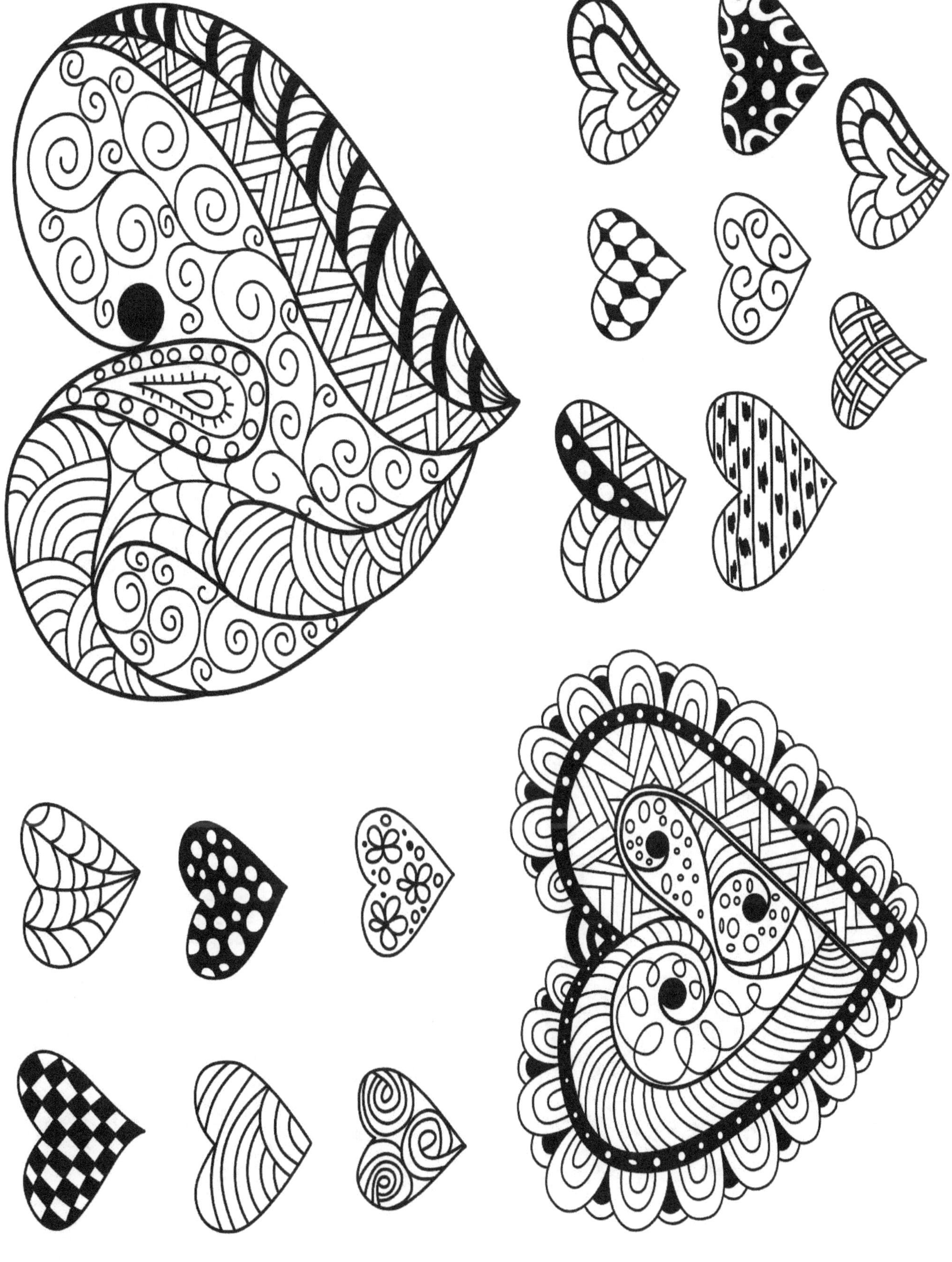

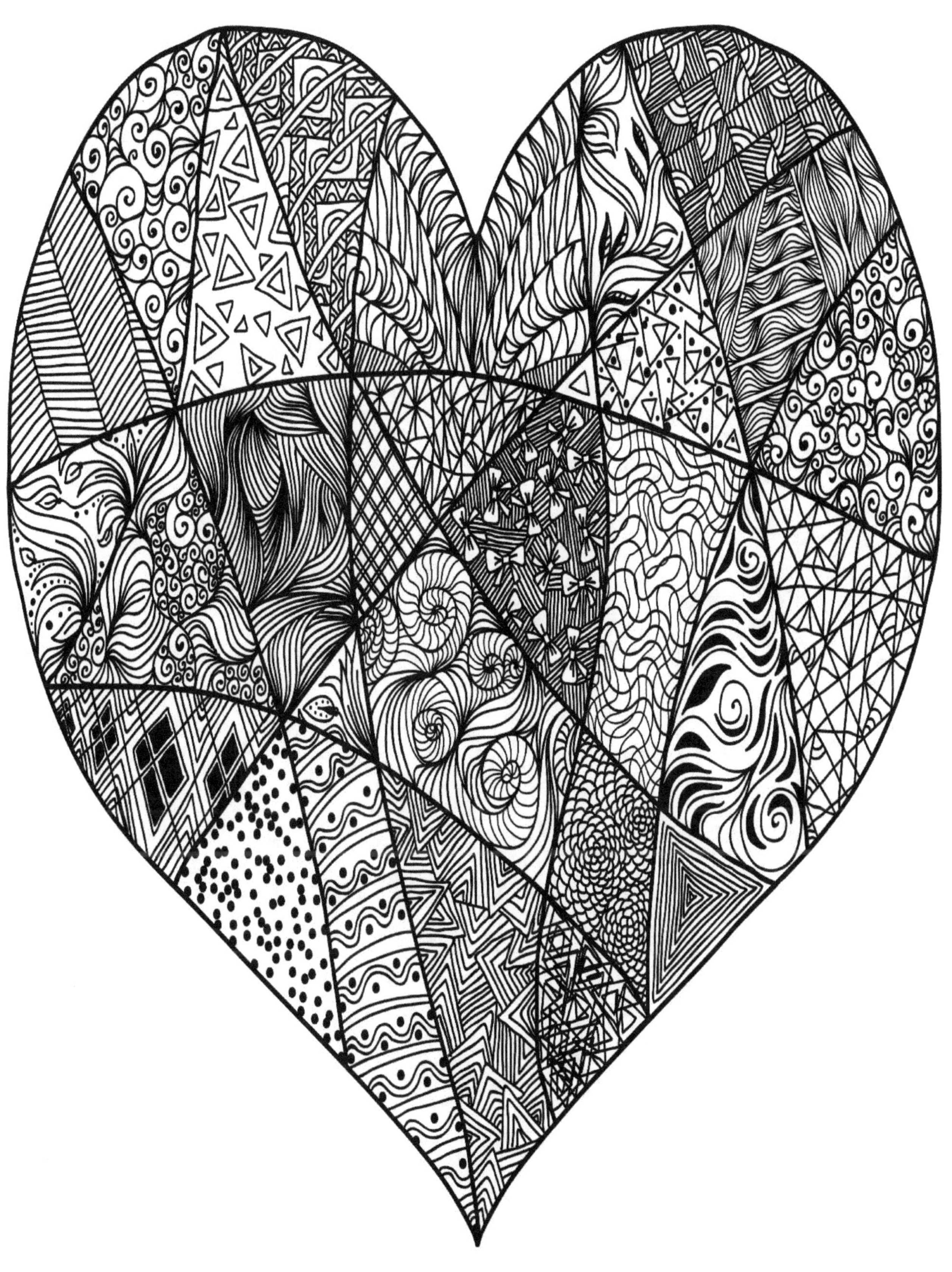

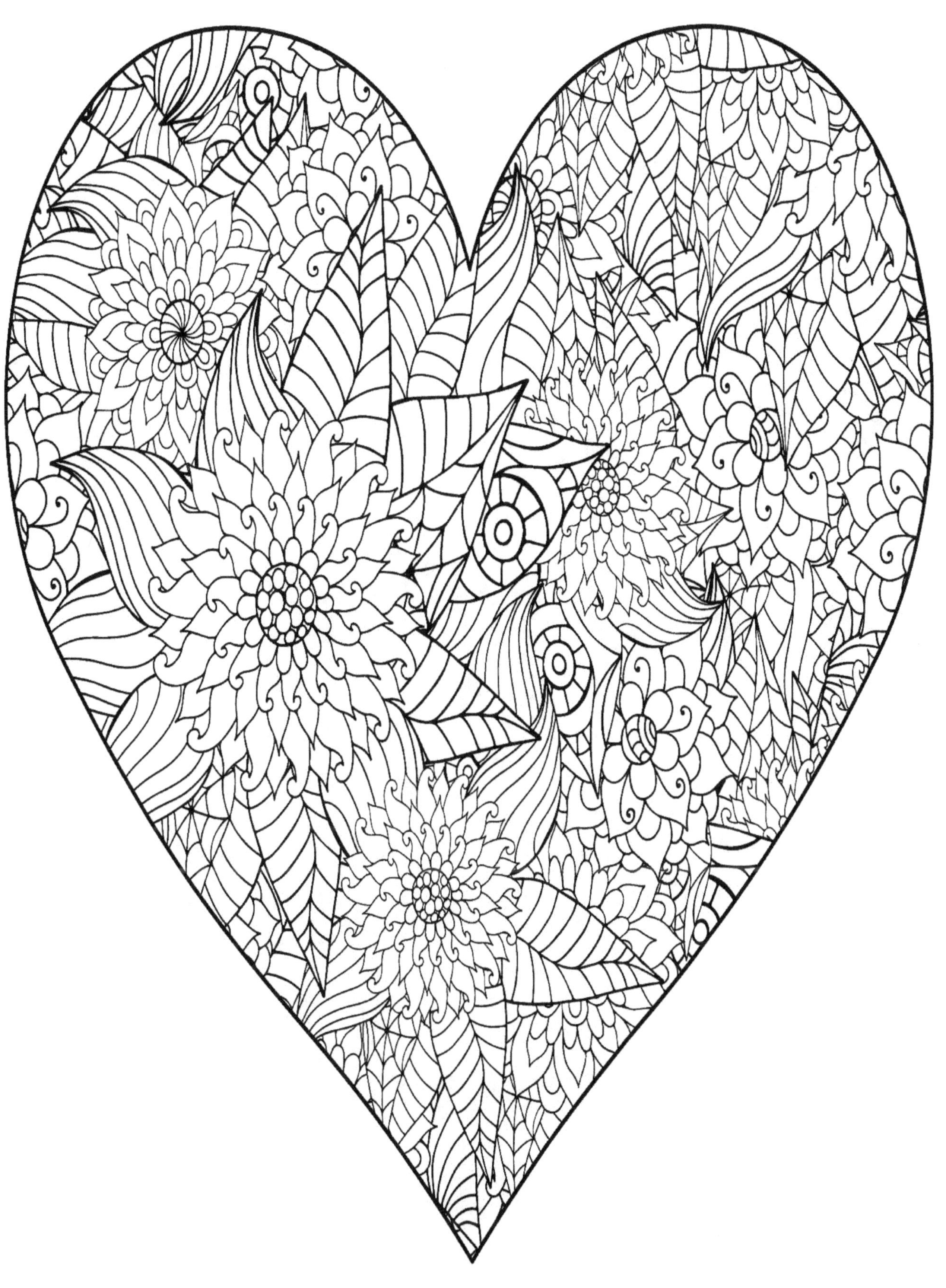

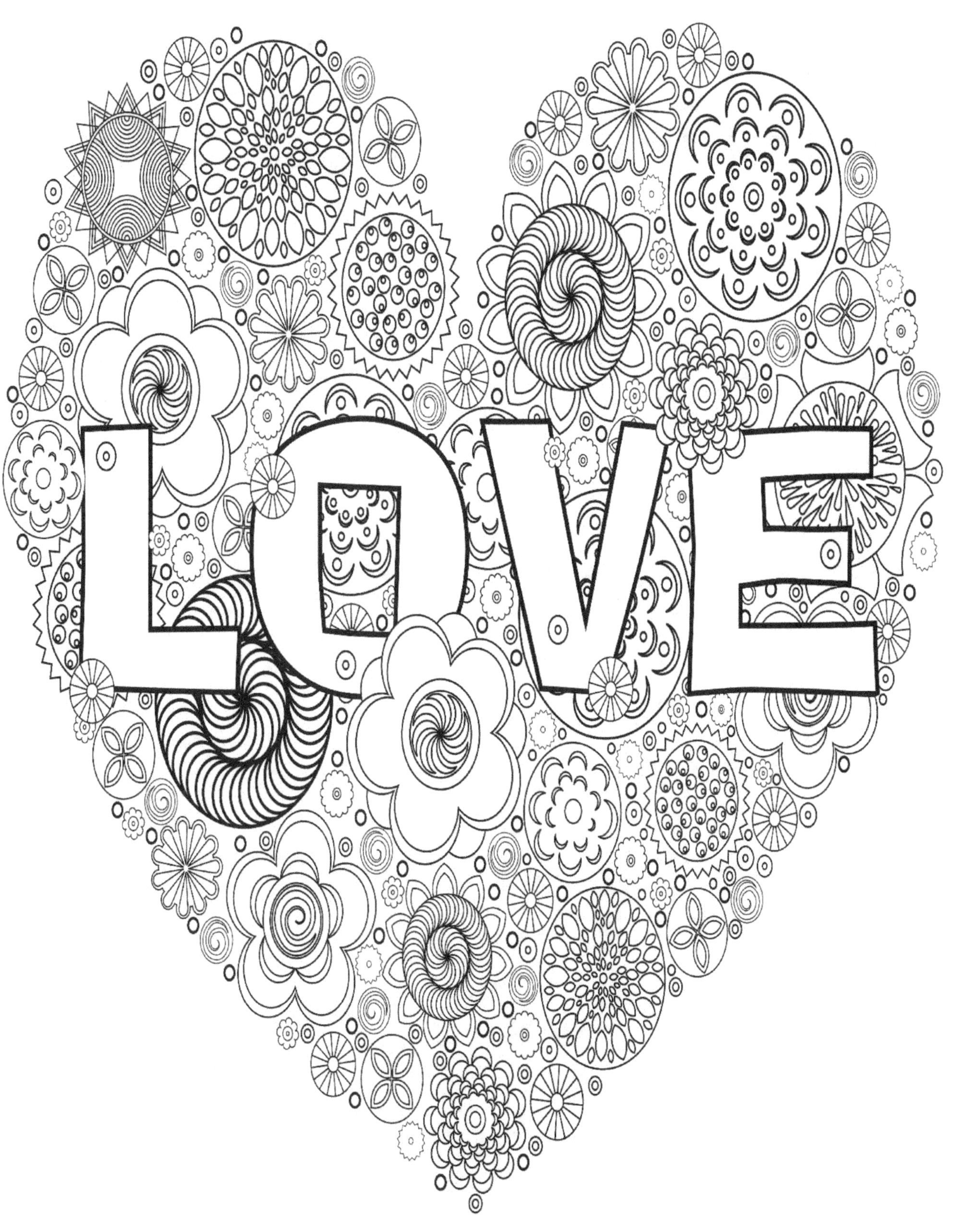
LOVE

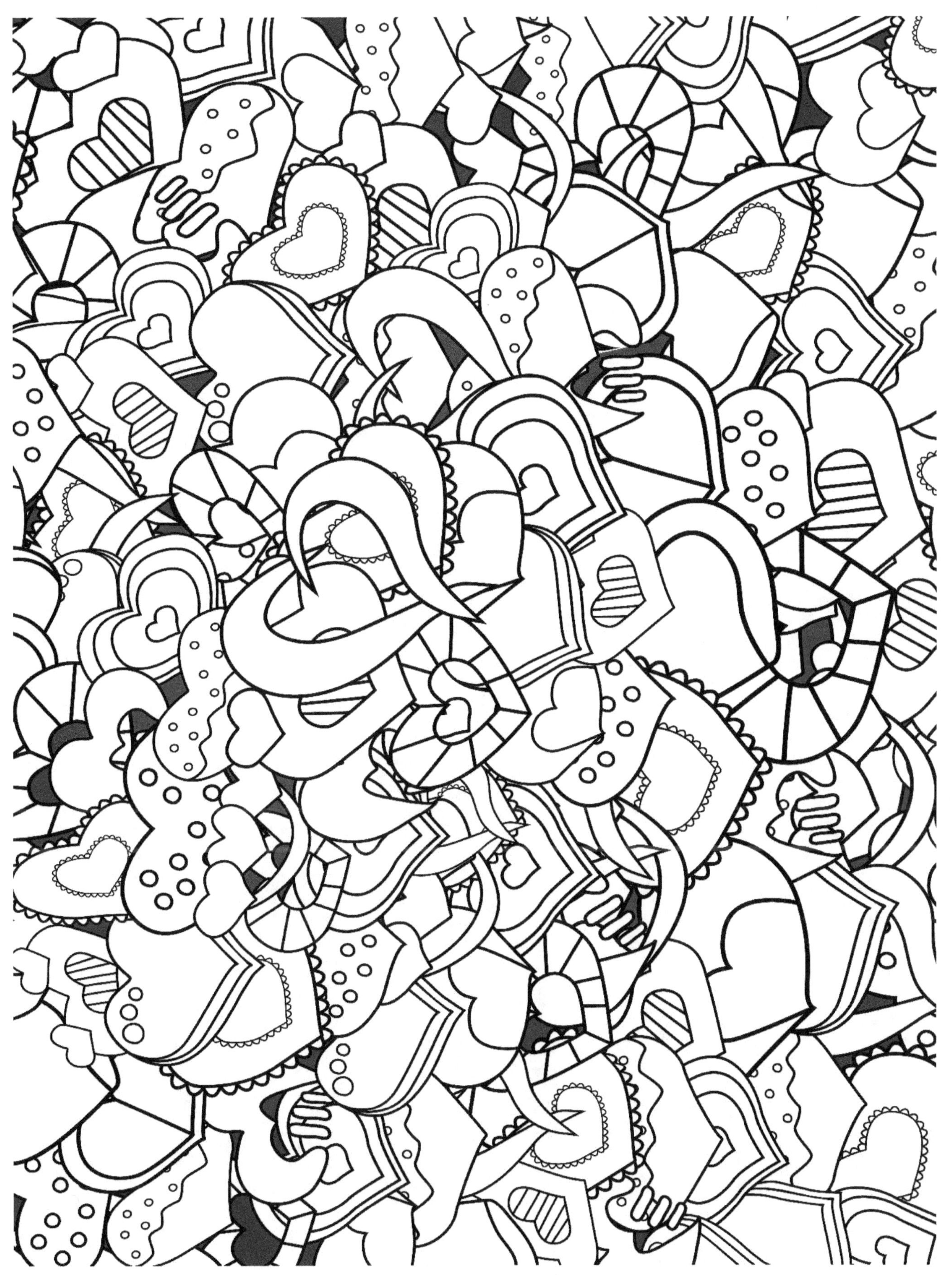

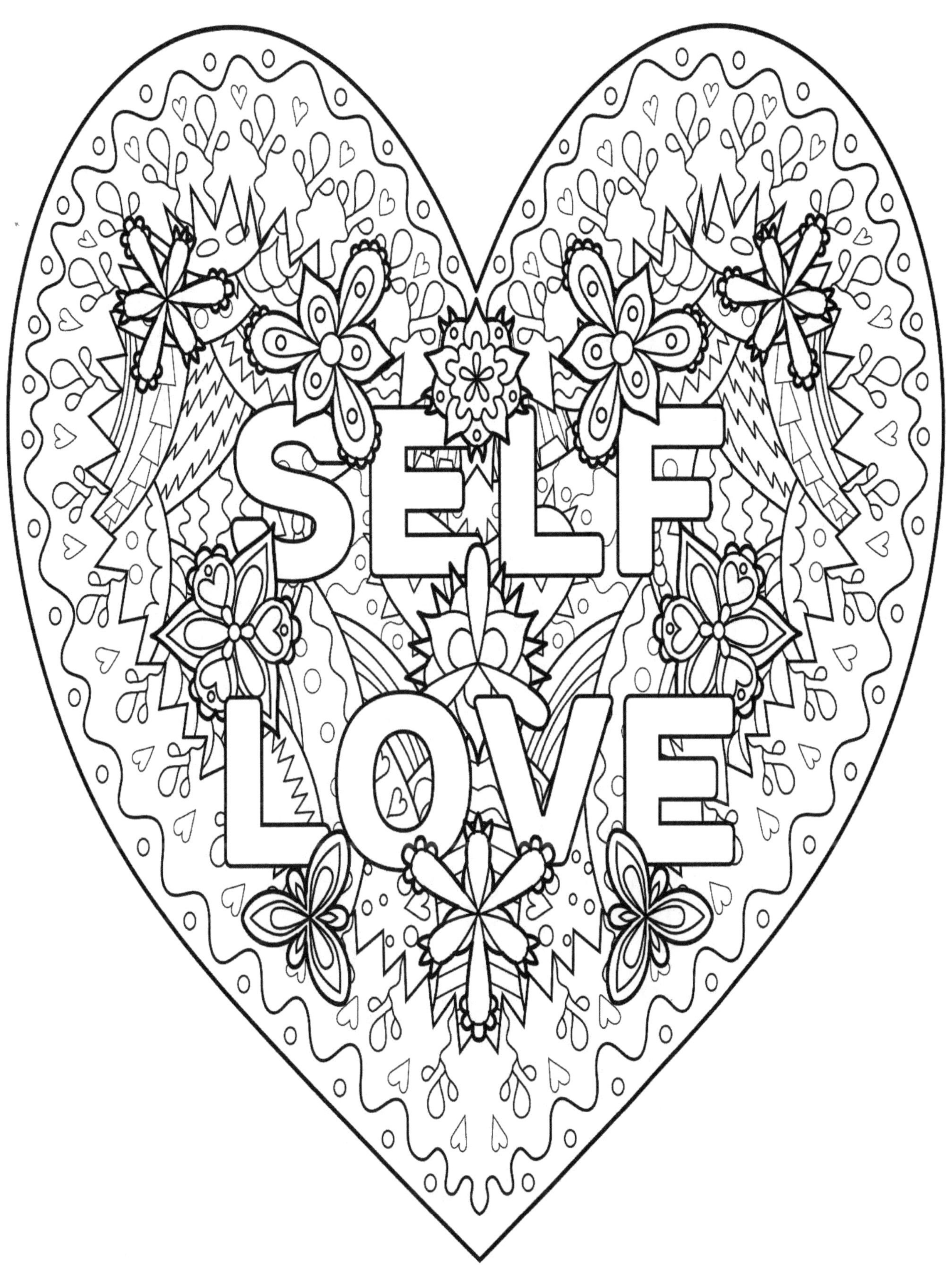
SELF
LOVE

About the Author:

Andrea Reynolds has always had an incredible imagination. She is the international bestselling author of over twenty five books. This is her fourth adult coloring book. She is the mother of two beautiful children, and one rescue dog. When not writing, her head will be found stuck in a book.

Also Available:

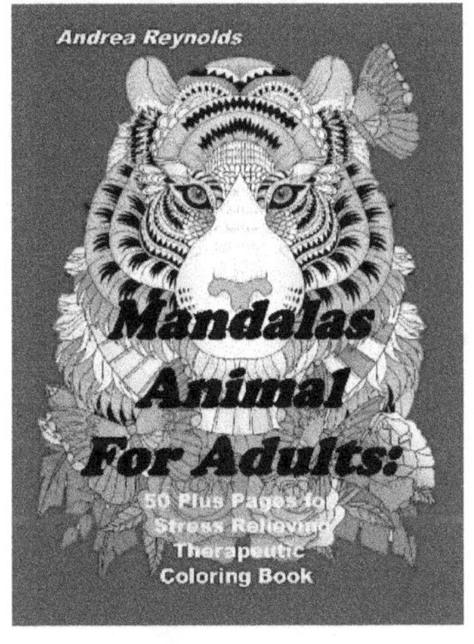

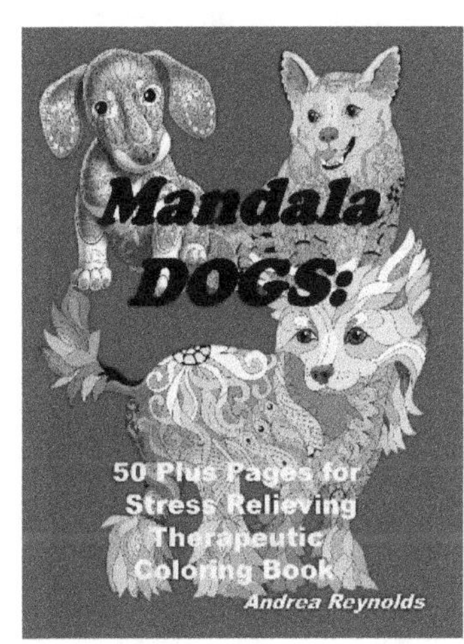

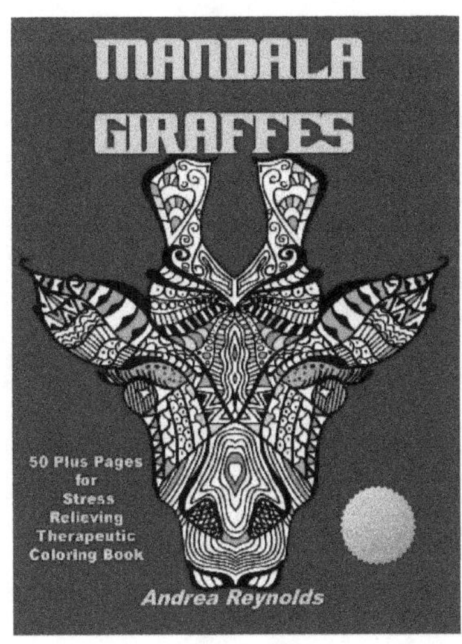

www.ingramcontent.com/pod-product-compliance
Lightning Source LLC
LaVergne TN
LVHW061204120826
845149LV00011B/1904
9781970106442